COWBOY
CAPITALISM

COWBOY CAPITALISM
European Myths, American Reality

◆

OLAF GERSEMANN

CATO INSTITUTE
Washington, D.C.

Originally published as *Amerikanische Verhältnisse: Die falsche Angst der Deutschen vor dem Cowboy-Kapitalismus,*
Copyright © 2003 FinanzBuch Verlag, Munich.
This English-language edition has been revised and expanded.

Library of Congress Cataloging-in-Publication Data

Gersemann, Olaf, 1968–
[Amerikanische Verhältnisse. English]
Cowboy capitalism : European myths, American reality /
Olaf Gersemann.
p. cm.
Includes bibliographical references.
ISBN 1-930865-62-7 (cloth: alk. paper)
ISBN 1-930865-78-3 (paper: alk. paper)
1. United States—Economic policy. 2. Europe—Economic policy. 3. United States—Economic conditions. 4. Europe—Economic conditions. 5. Capitalism—United States.
6. Capitalism—Europe. I. Title.

HC103.G4713 2004
330.973—dc22

2004057035

Cover design by Parker Wallman.

Printed in the United States of America.

CATO INSTITUTE
1000 Massachusetts Ave., N.W.
Washington, D.C. 20001
www.cato.org

Contents

PART III: UNEQUAL AND UNJUST

Acknowledgments

A few acknowledgments are in order: First, to Tom G. Palmer of the Cato Institute, whose relentless enthusiasm is the sole reason this book is published at all. To Elizabeth Kaplan, also of the Cato Institute, the most thorough copyeditor with whom I have ever had the pleasure of working. And to Jens Laurson, who, as the translator, rose to the challenge of bringing into plain English what was originally written in the language that, according to Mark Twain, "only the dead have time to learn."

For the generous assistance in the research of this book, I would like to acknowledge numerous staffers of the Deutsche Bundesbank, the Institut für Arbeitsmarkt- und Berufsforschung, the Organization for Economic Cooperation and Development, the Statistisches Bundesamt, the U.S. Bureau of Labor Statistics, and the U.S. Census Bureau; of particular help was the support of Nicole Le Vourch of the OECD and Cato Institute interns Linda Peia and Tudor Rus.

I also extend thanks to my parents, Marianne and Karl Gersemann, and a number of friends who volunteered to review drafts of the German version of this book: Birgit Braunwieser, Carter Dougherty, Monika Dunkel, Frank Engels, Michael Freitag, Michaela Hoffmann, Matthias Hohensee, Marc Hujer, Jaenene Lairo, Sandra Louven, Amy Medearis, Heidi Nadolski, Christoph Neßhöver, Laure Redifer, Carsten Rolle, Markus Steingröver, Stefan Sullivan, Olaf Unteroberdörster, Silke Wettach, Jobst Wiskow, and Jörg Zeuner. I have benefited hugely from their skepticism and suggestions.

Finally, I am indebted to my editor-in-chief, Stefan Baron, and his deputy, Klaus Methfessel, for their support of my bookwriting endeavors.

Abbreviations

AMA	American Medical Association
BEA	Bureau of Economic Analysis (U.S. Department of Commerce)
BJS	Bureau of Justice Statistics (U.S. Department of Justice)
BLS	U.S. Bureau of Labor Statistics (U.S. Department of Labor)
CEPR	Centre for Economic Policy Research
EITC	Earned Income Tax Credit
GDR	German Democratic Republic
ICT	Information and communication technologies
IMF	International Monetary Fund
IRS	Internal Revenue Service (U.S. Department of the Treasury)
JEC	Joint Economic Committee (U.S. Congress)
NBER	National Bureau of Economic Research
OECD	Organization for Economic Cooperation and Development
PPP	purchasing power parities
SVR	Sachverständigenrat zur Begutachtung der gesamtwirtschaftlichen Entwicklung (Germany)

Introduction

Over the last 25 years the U.S. economy has enjoyed an average annual real growth rate of 2.9 percent. That's 55 percent more than the German economy mustered, 48 percent more than in France, and 39 percent more than in the European Union as a whole.[1] In addition, none of the large European countries gets nearly as close to full employment as does the United States.

But if you think America's economy is considered a beacon, a role model for economic reform across continental Europe, you'd better think again.

Take Germany, for example. When Roland Koch, the minister president of the German state of Hesse and a leading conservative in German politics, suggested a couple of years ago that welfare reforms in Wisconsin might deserve a closer look, he faced a wave of public indignation.

Nowadays most politicians in continental Europe acknowledge the need for economic reform. Furthermore, since the mid-1990s looking abroad for best practices in economic policy has become an increasingly popular exercise in European countries, including Germany. Such benchmarking exercises, however, are in almost all cases restricted to continental European countries. German politicians, social scientists, and media usually look across the border to the Netherlands or Denmark—but not much further.

Almost never mentioned as a benchmark is the United States; Koch's suggestion was a very rare exception. To the contrary, in the economic policy debate across continental Europe, the U.S. economy serves as a popular bogeyman.

In Germany politicians regularly refer to *amerikanische Verhältnisse*. There's no precise translation for that term. It roughly means "American conditions" or "the way things are in America," and it is used in a derogatory way.

Gerhard Schröder, Germany's Social Democratic chancellor, for instance, says: "I do not want American conditions in the labor market. Social democrats are convinced that it has to be possible for people to live in decency and dignity without having to do three jobs a day and without any protection against dismissal."[2]

Opposition leaders take a similar stand. Edmund Stoiber, the minister president of Bavaria, who ran against Schröder as the conservative candidate in the 2002 federal elections, declares: "Employees and their families also need security. We do not want American conditions in Germany."[3]

Or take Guido Westerwelle, chairman of the Free Democrats, who like to portray themselves as Germany's most libertarian party. "I am," Westerwelle says, "far away from suggesting importing the so-called American conditions to Germany—precisely because I know them very well."[4]

Even business executives don't want to come across as sympathetic to American-style capitalism. Kajo Neukirchen, who has been CEO of several large German manufacturing companies, is a good example. Although the media consider him Germany's toughest top executive, he does "not want American conditions, with hiring and firing being the order of the day. Three jobs at the same time just to make a living—you don't want that and neither do I."[5]

Why exactly "American conditions" are something to be feared is never explained in detail. Implicitly, however, the following claim is made: U.S.-style "cowboy capitalism" might create a bit more economic growth and a few more jobs, but Americans pay a huge price in income inequality and other social problems.

This book presents the facts and demonstrates how misleading are such claims about "American conditions." As indicated above, the cost attached to Euro-style "comfy capitalism" in terms of growth and job creation has become huge over the last decades. And it's not at all clear that the United States does worse with regard to factors such as equal opportunity and income security.

This book doesn't claim that the performance of the U.S. economy has been spectacular in recent decades or that America's social problems are nonexistent. The message is simple: While U.S.-style capitalism may or may not have delivered results to be proud of, its performance, as measured by economic and social indicators, has clearly been superior to that of its continental European counterparts. In other words, the price Americans are paying for the benefits of their cowboy capitalism is surprisingly small, and it is likely that, if Europeans decided to Americanize their economic systems, they would gain much more than they would lose.

An earlier version of this book was published in October 2003 by FinanzBuch Verlag, Munich, as *Amerikanische Verhältnisse. Die falsche Angst der Deutschen vor dem Cowboy-Kapitalismus* (American Conditions: Why Germans Are Wrong to Fear Cowboy Capitalism).

This edition is a revised and updated version that does not limit itself to German-American comparisons but also includes France and Italy—two other big continental European economies—as well.

France and Italy have been chosen since they, along with Germany, are better suited for transatlantic comparisons than, say, the European Union as a whole. That's because an EU-U.S. comparison would include countries such as Ireland or Portugal whose economic characteristics—at least up until rather recent years—in many ways resembled those of emerging markets more than those of mature industrialized countries. Such a comparison would also include the fourth European heavyweight, the United Kingdom, whose economic system nowadays is arguably closer to American-style capitalism than to capitalism's "Rhineland" version.

In any case, France, Germany, and Italy, taken together, represent a very large part of the European economy. In 2003 they accounted for 48 percent of the EU's economic output and for 61 percent of the smaller euro zone's GDP.[6]

* * *

Part I of this book looks at the development of economic growth, employment, and productivity on both sides of the Atlantic and searches for the reasons for the divergences that emerge.

The analysis focuses on performance since the late 1970s for three reasons. First, because if one took a glance at only the last couple of years, longer-term trends might be overshadowed by short-term cyclical swings. Second, the shorter the time span examined, the more an international comparison can be distorted by so-called asymmetric shocks. For instance, the costly reunification of Germany could well be responsible for the lackluster economic performance of the country since 1990. But if it turns out that Germany had problems keeping up with the U.S. economy long before the Berlin Wall fell, that explanation becomes far less convincing.

Third, the second half of the 1970s marks an important economic turning point. The revolution in information and communication technologies that got under way then is likely to be one of the key reasons for the transatlantic divergence of many economic indicators.

Part II looks at the prejudices about and stereotypes of the American economy that are common in Europe. Some of the quotes above, for instance, indicate that it is commonly believed in Germany that many Americans must work two or three jobs to make a living.

Other stereotypes, too, enter the realm of public discussion all the time: that average families can maintain their living standard only because both parents work; that, as an influential German news magazine put it, "prosperity in the U.S. . . . is *for the most part* debt-financed";[7] or that the U.S. unemployment rate is so low only because so many people are behind bars.

American reality, however, looks quite different. Some of the prejudices, as it turns out after a closer look, are simply myths. Others have some truth to them, but in those cases it is often doubtful that the fact that U.S.-style capitalism is relatively unrestrained is the main factor behind the underlying social problems.

Of course, the stereotypes mentioned are not figments of only the European imagination. That poverty is on the rise in America or that the middle class is disappearing might seem credible to any regular American reader of the *New York Times.*

But the willingness to buy into such statements uncritically is much greater in Europe. "We'll be lucky if they let us cut back to forty hours a week when we're eighty-two, or incontinent, whichever comes first," writes author Michael Moore in his book *Stupid White Men.*[8] With juicy quotes of that kind, Moore made it onto the bestseller list in the United States, but his success was far greater in Germany.

For months on end, *Stupid White Men* was the best-selling nonfiction book there. By early 2004, according to Moore himself, "over three million copies [had] sold worldwide."[9] The German-language edition alone, according to its publisher, had found 1.4 million buyers.[10]

4

Stupid White Men did eventually slip into second place in the German sales rankings. It was replaced at the top by *Dude, Where's My Country?*—by Michael Moore.

Part III is devoted to economic justice and security in the United States and how America compares with France, Germany, and Italy.

This part of the book faces the difficulty that something like economic justice is harder to measure than economic growth or unemployment rates. What exactly is "just," to begin with? When every member of society receives a share of prosperity that is proportional to his or her individual contribution or effort? When everyone has equal opportunities? Or when differences in income and wealth that the forces of supply and demand naturally create are evened out in the end? Depending on personal preferences, the answers will vary.

Therefore, the results of American-European comparisons, too, are prone to be interpreted and weighted differently. However, as Part III shows, it would be a bold assertion to say that these results clearly speak in favor of countries such as France, Germany, or Italy.

* * *

A few words about the methodology used: This book is based for the most part on (freely available) statistics. Of course, relying on statistics has its limitations. Numbers can give a skewed or entirely distorted picture. Furthermore, many statistics offer much room for interpretation. After all, whether the glass is half full or half empty is a matter of perspective.

Furthermore, international comparisons present the danger of comparing apples with oranges. Unemployment, for example, is measured differently in the United States and in Europe. To attain a minimum of comparability, data from institutions such as the Paris-based Organization for Economic Cooperation and Development are preferred; that method at times comes at the cost of timeliness.

Where sources are given as Internet URLs, the cited information can be found on the websites of the quoted institutions or persons; wherever a citation is neither a URL nor a bibliographical reference, the quoted institution or person provided the information upon request.

PART I

HE WHO LAUGHS LAST—EMPLOYMENT IN EUROPE
AND THE UNITED STATES, 1979–2003

1. The End of Convergence

A head of state speaks of a national malaise. A "crisis of confidence" has grasped the people, he proclaims in a famous speech given on July 15, 1979. That crisis "is threatening to destroy the social and political fabric" of the country.

The country in question is the United States of America and the president is Jimmy Carter. The crisis of which Carter speaks has partly political causes. The humiliating retreat from Vietnam and the Watergate scandal especially have left their marks on the collective consciousness of the country.

The country is in dire straits economically as well. Japan's exporters have started their move into the U.S. market. Within four years, Honda, Toyota, and others double their share of the U.S. car market to 20 percent. By the end of 1979, only a billion-dollar loan guaranteed by the federal government can save Chrysler, once an icon of America's economic might, from going under.

Leading U.S. economists resign themselves to the idea that high inflation and low growth rates are unavoidable for America. Nobel Prize–winning economist Paul Samuelson, for example, predicts that in the 1980s America will witness average annual inflation of 9 percent and more than 8 percent unemployment; he expects the annual growth rate of gross domestic product to be barely 2 percent. And that makes Samuelson almost one of the optimists of the time.[1] At first, it seemed as though Samuelson was going to be right. In the early 1980s, Americans suffered two massive, consecutive recessions.

Modell Deutschland Still Alive

A slew of European countries also found themselves in crisis in the late 1970s. Double-digit inflation rates became the rule in Italy, and things didn't look much better in France.

But at least West Germany still seemed to enjoy what had been dubbed the *Wirtschaftswunder*—the economic miracle that had started shortly after the end of World War II. The golden decades

9

after the war came to an end even for Germany with the oil-price crisis in 1973–74. After that the unemployment rate never again had a zero as its first digit. Consumer prices rose almost a third in five years. And the federal budget slipped into the red.

Still, the thought of looking abroad for advice on economic policy seemed downright silly to Germans. Compared with other industrialized countries, West Germany in the second half of the 1970s was paradise—or so it seemed. After all, unemployment and inflation rates were three times higher in the United States. Chancellor Helmut Schmidt proudly praised the *Modell Deutschland* during the campaign before the 1976 federal elections—and was promptly reelected.

Catching Up

It's almost natural for poor countries to catch up with richer ones. Consider the following example. Give a dirt-poor farmer a plow worth $100 and he may possibly double or triple his harvest. A somewhat wealthier farmer who already owns a plow and an ox may also invest $100 well. He may buy better feed for the ox or superior seed for his fields. He, too, will likely increase his yield— but not as dramatically as the poor farmer. A rich farmer, finally, who has seed, fertilizer, pesticides, and herbicides as well as all modern machinery available, will also find a profitable way to invest $100. That this investment will, however, produce any more than a marginal increase in yield is unlikely.

Economists therefore speak of "decreasing returns to scale." In production processes of all kinds, the lower your capital stock is to start with, the greater the growth rate you can achieve with additional capital. That phenomenon can be seen in the global economy as well: developing countries can achieve higher economic growth rates than emerging countries; and emerging countries manage to grow faster than industrialized countries—at least if and when there are no obstacles to cross-border flows of capital and know-how. Economists call this a "catch-up effect." Theoretically, poor countries should catch up with richer ones—living standards should converge and worldwide inequalities should recede, not grow.

The process of convergence might be very slow, especially if rich countries compensate for diminishing returns with efficient usage of technological advances. Success, on the other hand, can be copied. In this sense the most developed countries resemble explorers who make their way through the jungle, leaving in their wake a path for others to follow. After all, products need be invented only once; and methods of production and industrial arrangements that prove successful can be imitated.

Indeed, countries that gave up autarky and socialist planning, managed to limit corruption, and enjoyed relatively stable political conditions caught up dramatically with the Western industrialized nations. In 1950 Korea was barely better off than India, and Japan had a per capita income just about comparable to Turkey's.[2] Today, Korea and Japan are among the richest countries in the world.

However, convergence is not guaranteed. It can be stunted significantly. Countries such as Afghanistan, Angola, Iraq, Cuba, Madagascar, Nicaragua, Niger, and Somalia had a lower per capita income in 1998 than they did in 1950.[3] Among the possible causes are adverse geographic conditions and a hot, humid climate that is conducive to diseases such as malaria.[4] But it seems to be primarily the political and institutional framework that is responsible for the success or failure of the process of convergence.[5] That in turn means that convergence even under good geographical circumstances is not a given. And even if convergence has gotten under way, there is nothing inevitable about it; it can still wane or even wither entirely.

Sadly, France, Germany, and Italy are good examples.

Falling Behind

In the mid-19th century, prosperity for the first time was greater in the United States than in the old world. And while the United States profited from its gigantic domestic market and its abundance of natural resources, Europe fell further and further behind. In 1950, after two devastating wars, Western Europe barely reached 56 percent of the American per capita income.[6]

What followed, however, was exactly what theory predicts. On the basis of purchasing power parities (i.e., exchange rates that eliminate the differences in price levels between countries), Europe caught up again. Converted to 1999 dollars, the 1960 per capita income of Germany was $10,925, almost 80 percent of the U.S. level at that time. In the 1960s and 1970s the French, Germans, and Italians continued to gain ground.

11

Figure 1.1
REAL GROSS DOMESTIC PRODUCT PER CAPITA IN FRANCE,
GERMANY, AND ITALY COMPARED WITH THE UNITED STATES
(CONVERTED TO U.S. DOLLARS USING PURCHASING POWER PARITIES,
UNITED STATES = 100)

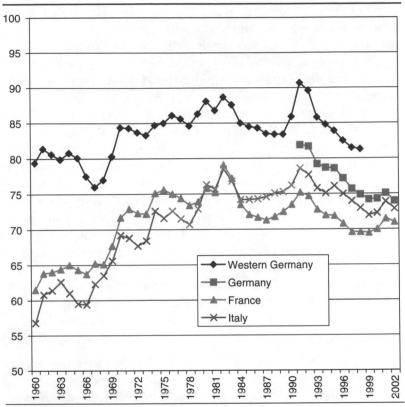

SOURCE: U.S. Bureau of Labor Statistics (2003), p. 10.

Europe did not catch up overnight, nor was its progress particularly steady. When, for instance, Lyndon B. Johnson's "guns and butter" policies in the late 1960s artificially boosted demand in America, Europeans ceded some of the ground gained earlier. In the end, however, the upward tendency was indisputable (Figure 1.1). By the early 1980s per capita GDP in France and Italy reached almost 80 percent of the U.S. level; in Germany it was close to 90 percent.

Since then, however, it's been all downhill for the French, Germans, and Italians. The process of convergence petered out. Convergence was replaced by divergence. This new trend, too, has been interrupted temporarily, most notably in the early 1990s when the United States suffered from a mild recession while Germany still enjoyed the brief economic boom caused by the fall of the Berlin Wall and reunification.

What remains true, though, is that the three big continental European countries *are* falling behind. By the late 1990s the gap in per capita income between Italy and the United States had widened to a size not seen since the late 1970s. In the cases of France and West Germany you even have to look back to the late 1960s to see a gap of that size in the statistics.

The price Europeans are paying for the end of convergence is considerable. Just consider the following hypothetical scenarios:

- Scenario one assumes that the trend of the 1960s and 1970s would have continued steadily between 1982 and 2002.
- Scenario two assumes that the convergence trend would have continued at half its previous speed after 1982.
- In scenario three the assumption is that the transatlantic gap in per capita incomes would have remained the same after 1982.

Had the first scenario become reality, in 2002 per capita income in France would have been 95.1 percent of that in the United States; in Italy it would have reached 98.2 percent (Figure 1.2). Calculated in 1999 dollars and using purchasing power parities, per capita income in France and Italy would have reached $32,694 and $33,770, respectively. Comparing those numbers to the actually realized levels of income yields the loss associated with the end of convergence after 1982. In the case of France, the loss amounts to $8,299 per capita; in the case of Italy, the amount is $8,715. These numbers refer to the year 2002 alone—the loss accumulated over the last 20 years is of course much higher.

To be fair, one could not expect the convergence process to continue at the same pace it did in the 1960s and 1970s. The principle of decreasing returns to scale suggests just that. As the economies of poorer countries pick up, one should see their growth rates slow down, just as growth in the richest countries has done before. Therefore, experts, if asked back in the early 1980s, would likely have considered scenario two the most realistic.

Figure 1.2

REAL GROSS DOMESTIC PRODUCT PER CAPITA IN FRANCE, ITALY,
AND THE UNITED STATES, 2002
(PURCHASING POWER PARITIES, 1999 DOLLARS)

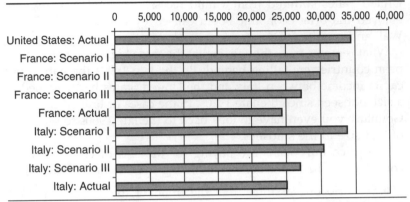

SOURCES: U.S. Bureau of Labor Statistics (2003), pp. 10–11; and author's calculations.

However, even in comparison with that scenario, reality turns out to be very dismal for France and Italy. The per capita income lost in 2002 because of the deviation of reality from scenario two stands at $5,549 and $5,324 for France and Italy, respectively.

Finally, consider the even more modest third scenario. That scenario would have become reality if continental European countries, after decades of catching up, suddenly and for whatever reason had stopped doing so—but without losing ground. Even under those circumstances, per capita incomes in 2002 would have been considerably higher. The difference in France would have been $2,799, and in Italy it would have been $1,933.

Germany is not part of those considerations because numbers for West Germany are available only through 1998. But here, too, the income loss that the end of convergence brought about is substantial. Calculated for 1998, the loss for every West German would be between $2,399 (scenario three) and $4,680 (scenario one).

A Closer Look at per Capita Income

What happened? When searching for the causes of the end of convergence, it's useful to look at the factors on which income depends.

By definition, per capita income is the product of

- the number of people employed relative to the size of the population,
- the annual hours worked per employed person, and
- the average value of output per hour worked (i.e., the productivity of labor).

The first two factors are obviously explained by what is going on in the labor market. A comparison of labor markets in the United States and the European countries will therefore be the focus of Chapter 2. Chapter 3 will then take a closer look at the development of the third factor, labor productivity.

2. Europe Isn't Working

The end of work is near!

That declaration was popularized by American writer Jeremy Rifkin in *The End of Work*. The main thrust of that 1995 book is that workers in industrialized countries are threatened with being rationalized out of the workforce. Three of four workers—or so Rifkin claimed—did work that could be automated.

That thesis was soon picked up on the other side of the Atlantic. The prominent German sociologist Ulrich Beck, for example, was quick to proclaim that "the Germans are too industrious." Therefore, "we are working ourselves superfluous." The solution he suggests is that men tend more to wives and children and that everybody be more concerned with volunteering. At any rate, the "straitjacket of full employment policies" ought to be cast off, Beck declared.[1]

Union leaders in continental Europe think along these lines: The demand for work is being depleted, or, at the very least, we can't increase it any further. Consequently, the existing amount of work should be distributed more fairly. Hence the demands for a mandatory 35- or even 30-hour workweek. Hence also top German trade union official Michael Sommer's remark that "workers who can afford to do so, should work less."[2]

Jeremy Rifkin and Ulrich Beck might just be on to something. Most of the jobs that exist today may well be automated in the course of innovation in areas such as information technologies.

But when the jobs of today disappear in France, Germany, or Italy, they can be replaced by new, better, and more convenient jobs. That at least is what history, economic logic, and recent developments in America have shown.

Ideas, Needs, and Work—All Unlimited

If Rifkin and the others were right, Americans and Europeans would already have worked themselves out of jobs—at the beginning of the 19th century. Back then more than half the population worked in agriculture. New crops, new fertilizers, and finally mechanization made possible steady and in the end enormous increases in efficiency. The number of people needed to feed the population sank continually. In rich countries today, only a very small percentage of the workforce is in agriculture.[3]

Yet we didn't run out of work. Technological progress eradicated jobs in agriculture, but at the same time large numbers of new jobs were created, mostly in the manufacturing sector. "The industrial revolution has produced new jobs in sectors that had neither existed prior to it nor been foreseeable for anyone," writes German economist Axel Börsch-Supan.[4]

But what if fewer and fewer people can supply the goods the citizens of wealthy countries need? Won't work disappear then?

That hardly seems likely. The most basic reason for this is that no matter how much work is available, it will always be scarce in relation to our needs. Nowhere can any evidence be found that human needs that can be satisfied through the use of labor have any upper limits. That may sound materialistic; after all, don't the citizens of rich countries already have everything they need?

Absolutely not! That becomes obvious when we look back and see what consumers did *not* have 25 years ago. Cars back then differed from today's models by a lot more than the lack of airbags and air conditioners. Instead of computers with Internet access, instead of CD burners and DVD players, instead of cell and cordless phones, people had typewriters, reel-to-reel tape recorders, and rotary phones. Mountain bikes and carving skis were unavailable, as were in-line skates. And Viagra was still a distant dream for many couples.

One reason our needs are practically unlimited is that we are often unaware of them. In 1979 hardly anyone would have missed the opportunity to browse in what had not even been invented yet but was later named the World Wide Web. Nowadays the Web seems like a part of the furniture of the modern world. Plenty of people would badly miss browsing the Net or communicating via e-mail.

But if human needs truly know no limits, then the only way in which we might run out of work is if mankind were to cease coming up with new ideas for satisfying all existent or latent needs. "Everything that can be invented has been invented," Charles Duell, then head of the U.S. Patent and Trademark Office, is quoted as having said in 1899.[5] So far, however, human inventiveness has not shown any signs of slowing down.

It's true that technological progress eliminates existing jobs. It will do so in the future, too. It's also true that finding a replacement for an old job is often hard and painful for the individual. Learning new skills or moving to a different region is difficult and costly.

When old jobs disappear, though, without new ones being created, it isn't technological progress that's to blame. When modern economies have to deal with high levels of unemployment over long periods of time, the reasons must lie elsewhere. Studying the United States since the early 1980s indicates that, indeed, they do.

Unemployment

Just a quarter of a century ago, unemployment was relatively high in the United States. In 1975 the unemployment rate in America was about twice that in France and Italy and close to three times the rate in Germany. Just nine years later, in 1984, unemployment rates in France and Italy rose above the U.S. level and have remained there ever since. Germany's unemployment rate has exceeded that of the United States since 1993 (Figure 2.1).[6]

At the height of the past economic boom, in April 2000, the U.S. unemployment rate sank to a record low of 3.8 percent. The last time such a low level had been reached was in 1969—during the Vietnam War. In peacetime, a lower level had been achieved only once in the past 50 years, in March 1957.

During the last recession, unemployment rose again. In the summer of 2003 it reached over 6 percent. That was the *highest* level for the United States since 1994.[7] For Germany, Italy, and France that level would have been the *lowest* since 1991, 1980, and 1979, respectively.

What's more, even prolonged economic upswings in the big European countries have ceased to bring unemployment down decisively. During peak years of cyclical upswings in the United States, the unemployment level went from 5.8 percent (1979) and 5.3 percent (1989) to 4.0 percent (2000). In Germany, in contrast, the cyclical lows went from 1.7 percent (1980) and 4.5 percent (1991) up to 7.3 percent (2000).

Employment

The official unemployment rate is the most common measure of what's going on in the labor market. At the same time, it's a rather

Figure 2.1
UNEMPLOYMENT RATES IN THE UNITED STATES, FRANCE, GERMANY, AND ITALY
(PERCENT)

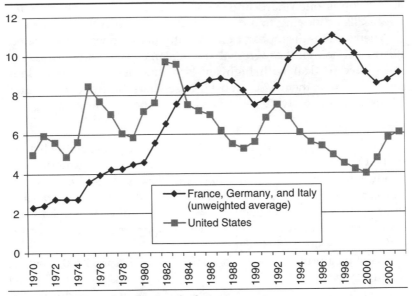

SOURCES: OECD and author's calculations.

insufficient one. If a German or American unemployed father frustrated with job hunting gives up looking for a job altogether and focuses on housework and children, then he is, according to the official statistics, no longer unemployed.

The unemployment rate can also be manipulated politically. Government-subsidized early retirement or "active" labor market measures are commonly used for such purposes in Europe. The number of jobs that exist solely thanks to targeted subsidies from the German government, for instance, tends to increase regularly before federal elections. In 2002 almost 1.75 million Germans dropped out of the unemployment statistics because of such state interventions. Had that "hidden" unemployment entered the statistics, the German unemployment rate in 2002 would have been 2.6 percentage points higher.[8]

To assess the job market performance of an economy, a closer look at the statistics is therefore necessary. One important indicator

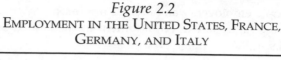

Figure 2.2
EMPLOYMENT IN THE UNITED STATES, FRANCE, GERMANY, AND ITALY

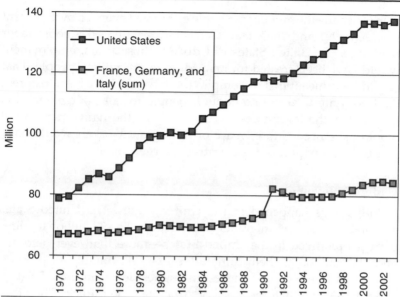

SOURCES: OECD and author's calculations.

is the number of employed persons. Figure 2.2 shows the changes in that number between 1970 and 2003 for the United States and for France, Germany, and Italy taken together. The figure shows the following:[9]

- Between 1970 and 2003 the number of people employed in the United States rose by 58.9 million. That's the equivalent of a 75 percent increase. In the three European countries, employment increased by fewer than 17.6 million people, or by 26 percent.
- Almost half the increase in Europe was due to German reunification. In 1991 alone, the first year in which the former German Democratic Republic (East Germany) enters the statistics, employment in the three countries, taken together, rose by 8.3 million.
- Growth in employment in Europe has been especially disappointing since the beginning of the 1990s. In 2003 the number

21

of people employed was only 2.2 million higher than in 1991. Over the same period, employment in the United States grew by 18.9 million.

In Germany the number of people employed even fell by .5 percent between 1991 and 2003. Had Germany experienced a boom labor market as the United States did during those years, employment would have been created for an additional 6.6 million people. That would have meant that full employment would have been restored. And not only that; to find enough people for all those 6.6 million jobs, either the labor force participation of the native population would have needed to increase or immigrant workers would have had to be brought into the country in larger numbers.

Underemployment

Both things happened in the United States. The United States accepted a wave of immigrants. In 2002 more than 33 million foreign-born people lived in the United States—more than ever before—and 15.7 million of them came after 1990. At roughly 12 percent, the share of immigrants reached its highest level since the 1930s.[10]

But that's only half the story of America's job miracle. The other half is that an increasing share of the working-age population is participating in the labor force. The share of employed persons as a percentage of the working-age population used to be 65 percent or less in the early 1970s (Figure 2.3). In the mid-1970s, however, the employment ratio started to rise. In 1987 it passed the 70 percent threshold and has remained above it ever since.

In 2000 the employment ratio reached an all-time high of 74.1 percent. Two years later, it had fallen back to 71.9 percent. Even at that level, it compares very well with continental European ratios. Although the employment ratio has risen in Italy over the last few years, it started at a dismally low level and reached a mere 55.6 percent in 2002.

Employment ratios in Germany and France are higher, but they are, if anything, trending downward. Thirty years ago the French ratio was about the same as the U.S. ratio. And while it's seen a small rise since 1997, at 62.2 percent it's still lower than it was 30 years ago. In the early 1970s the German employment ratio considerably exceeded the American level. In 2002, however, it was only 65.2—

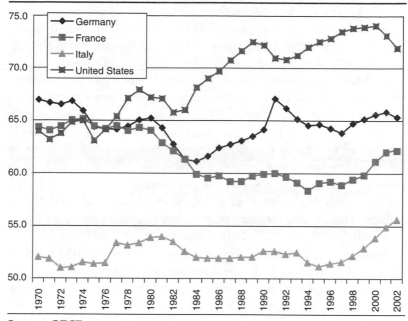

Figure 2.3
EMPLOYMENT RATIOS IN THE UNITED STATES, FRANCE,
GERMANY, AND ITALY
(EMPLOYED PERSONS BETWEEN 15 AND 64 YEARS OF AGE AS A
PERCENTAGE OF WORKING-AGE POPULATION)

SOURCE: OECD.

far below the ratio in the United States. That's all the more remark-able since reunification jolted that ratio in the early 1990s, thanks to the traditionally high female labor force participation in the for-mer GDR.

Whatever the causes, a large minority of the working-age popula-tion being out of work is a gigantic waste of human capital. Knowl-edge and skills that people amassed over years remain untapped. That's the case in the United States, but it's much more so in the continental European countries.

Time Worked

Unemployment rates, the number of unemployed people, and em-ployment ratios don't reveal the whole extent of underemployment in France, Germany, and Italy. The whole misery comes to light only when one also considers the amount of time actually worked. That's important because it turns out that those who are still working in Europe are working less and less.

European countries have cut their workweeks down considerably. In France and Germany, labor unions, with some success, fought for a 35-hour week. In addition, an increasing share of people employed in Europe don't have full-time jobs. In the United States, part-time employment as a share of total employment was slightly lower in 2002 than it had been in 1990. In Italy, on the other hand, the incidence of part-time employment had risen by 12 percent since 1990. In France and Germany the surge was even more pronounced, at 34 and 40 percent, respectively.[11]

To see what that implies, it helps to take a closer look at Germany. According to official German statistics, the aggregate number of employed persons rose by 595,000 between 1996 and 2003. As it turns out, however, the number of part-time employees rose by 2.7 million, while the number of full-time employees declined by 2.1 million. Thus, if you measure employment by full-time equivalents, it actually went down by slightly more than one million jobs.[12]

Before proceeding further into the matter, a few words of caution: all of the following statistics and calculations ought to be considered not precise numbers but comparisons of trends over time.[13] The bottom line, however, is that in the three European countries considered, people are working fewer hours. In 1970 people worked about 1,900 hours a year on both sides of the Atlantic (Figure 2.4). After 1970 the number of actual annual hours worked in the United States declined to a level as low as 1,806 hours (1982) but never fell below the 1,800-hour mark.

Not so in Europe: The reduction in hours worked continued throughout the 1980s and 1990s. In 2002 the average Italian worked only 1,619 hours; in France and Germany the averages were as low as 1,459 and 1,444 hours a year. By comparison, in 2002 the average employed person in America worked some 1,815 hours.

Falling employment ratios paired with dwindling hours worked mean that the hours worked per working-age person must have decreased in Europe. And so they did. The reduction was most pronounced in France and Germany. In 1970 the hours worked per calendar day and working-age person stood at 3.4 hours in France

Figure 2.4
Hours Worked in the United States, France, Germany, and Italy, per Annum and per Employed Person
(actual hours worked)

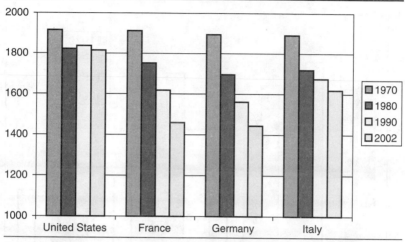

Source: OECD.

and 3.5 in Germany—slightly more than in the United States (Figure 2.5). In 2002, however, the numbers were 2.5 and 2.6 for France and Germany. The end of work was near! Were Rifkin, Beck, and Co. right, after all?

Well, no. At least in the United States, the increased employment ratio more than made up for the slight reduction in annual hours worked. At 3.6 hours per day per working-age person, the number was higher in 2002 than in 1970 or 1980.

It's Productivity, Stupid

In the continental European countries examined, a small part of the working-age population is working—and those people who are working are working less and less. The question arises of whether that trend is sustainable.

Perhaps it is. But the industrial countries are at the beginning of a decades-long demographic aging process. Because of low birthrates, France, Germany, and Italy in particular are hit much harder than is the United States. For instance, the United Nations predicts

Figure 2.5
HOURS WORKED IN THE UNITED STATES, FRANCE, GERMANY, AND ITALY, PER DAY AND PER PERSON BETWEEN 15 AND 64 YEARS OF AGE

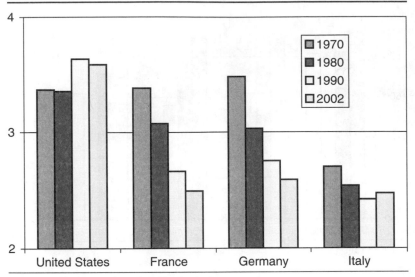

SOURCES: OECD and author's calculations.

that the share of 15- to 64-year-olds in the Italian population will decrease from 67 percent in 2002 to 53 percent in 2050. In the United States the reduction will be considerably less—from 67 to 60 percent.

That means that a smaller portion of the population will have to work for the prosperity of all. Consider the following example. If the actual hours worked and the total population are put into relation, the French, Germans, and Italians worked between 1.6 and 1.7 hours per person per day in 2002. In the United States the number was 2.5 hours, more than 40 percent higher (Figure 2.6).

Let's assume that the trend toward fewer hours worked was to stop and both the number of annual hours worked and the employment ratio remained the same for years to come. In that case, demographic aging would by 2050 have led to a 9 percent reduction in hours worked per day and per capita in the United States. In France, Germany, and Italy, the decline would be considerably larger—minus 12, minus 16, and minus 22 percent, respectively. In Italy, for

Figure 2.6
Hours Worked in the United States, France, Germany, and Italy, per Day and per Capita
(Assuming Constant Employment Ratios and Annual Hours Worked per Employed Person)

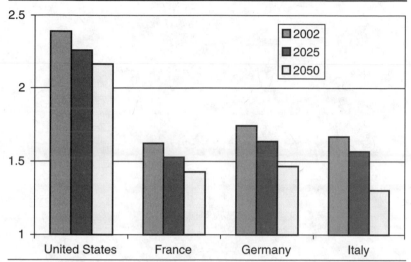

Sources: OECD (2003b), pp. 73, 169, 179, 219; United Nations (2000), pp. 232, 244, 282, 462; and author's calculations.

instance, the amount of work per day and person would be 80 minutes in 2050.

That means that either the European countries will have to experience reductions in their material standards of living or demographic aging will be compensated for by a return to longer working weeks and higher employment ratios.

The third alternative is that the remaining hours worked will be used more efficiently. In other words, "It's the productivity, stupid."

In that light, it's all the more worrisome that here, as the following chapter shows, Europe is falling far behind, too.

3. The New Economy Lives . . . In America

On average, a working-age German works about 2 hours and 35 minutes per calendar day. For her French and Italian neighbors, the working day is even shorter (see Chapter 2). Nations whose people work that little could raise their material living standards rather easily, simply by working longer hours.

In the long run, though, increasing prosperity can stem from only one source, increased labor productivity. When output grows, there can be just two causes: Either the input of work is increased, for example because the employed work overtime, because the jobless find work, or because the workforce grows as a result of high immigration or fertility rates. Or labor productivity increases, that is, the output per hour worked goes up.[1]

However, the workday can't be lengthened endlessly, and although unemployment can, theoretically at least, fall to zero, it can fall no lower. Only labor productivity can be increased indefinitely.

Labor Productivity Is Key

High productivity growth ensures that wages can grow fast without unit labor costs and inflation spiraling out of control. Workers in America are richer than their predecessors a hundred years ago, not because they work more (they don't) but because they are so much more productive.

With regard to productivity, in the long run every tenth of a percent counts. An example: Adjusted for purchasing power parities, per capita income in the United States was at 140 percent of the European Union average in 2002 (not counting the 2004 accession countries). If productivity growth in the United States had been one percentage point lower annually since World War II, America's per capita income would now be at 80 percent of the European level. The United States would not be richer than every European country (with the exemption of tiny Luxembourg) but instead would be poorer

trending down ever since the end of the short boom reunification brought. While labor productivity in the United States, as mentioned, grew by 3.09 percent between 1996 and 2003, Germany had to make do with 1.60 percent.

That divergence is significant. At a constant level of labor input, an annual labor productivity growth rate of 3.09 percent would imply a doubling of per capita income within 23 years. A country where the rate is only 1.60 percent achieves an increase of only 44 percent over the same period.

Looking at it from a different angle, in 2003 GDP per capita in the United States reached 142 percent of the German level (adjusted for differences in price levels); if the United States were to enjoy 23 more years with an annual increase in labor productivity of 3.09 percent while the growth rate in Germany remained at 1.60 percent, the gap between the two countries would widen to 196 percent by 2026.[10]

That discrepancy is counterintuitive. One would have expected higher gains in Germany:

- The reconstruction of East Germany (see Chapter 4) should have caused increased growth in productivity.
- Traditionally, the highest productivity growth can be attained in manufacturing, which accounts for a much higher proportion of GDP in Germany than in the United States (see Chapter 4).[11]
- In the job creation boom of the last two decades, labor force participation in the United States increased significantly. Especially immigrants and women were integrated into the workforce. Those groups tend to lower the level of productivity because they have, on average, either less education (immigrants) or less work experience (women). In 2002, for instance, roughly a third of foreign-born citizens had no high school diploma; among natives, the share is 13 percent.[12] In Germany, by contrast, the trend is for less-qualified workers to be pushed out of the workforce. That has, statistically, a positive effect on the level of productivity because only those workers who are actually employed enter the calculations.

Experts by now generally agree on the reasons for America's new productivity miracle. The progress in information and communication technologies (ICT)—for example, computers, software, the

Internet, and fiber optic networks—brought about a "new economy." Not only did ICT-producing industries realize astounding productivity increases; ICT users, too, were able to translate their investments into substantial increases in efficiency. The U.S. service sector in particular enjoyed high productivity growth. This is remarkable since it is often assumed that the potential for increasing productivity in the production of services is limited. That, if correct, would condemn high-income countries to sluggish GDP growth since consumption shifts toward services as economies mature—a phenomenon known as "Baumol's disease."[13]

That this disease seems to have been cured in the United States while other countries still suffer from it is not astounding if you consider how quickly ICT were adopted in America: The United States started investing in ICT earlier and more intensely than most European countries. In 1990 the ICT's share of total investment was 21.9 percent—a share that neither Germany nor France nor Italy reached even in 2001 (Figure 3.2).

The Solow Paradox

"We see the computer age everywhere except in the productivity statistics." That famous 1987 quote from Nobel laureate Robert Solow describes the astonishment of economists at the seemingly small effects ICT initially had on growth in productivity.

With hindsight, we are all smarter. It has since become the consensus among experts in the field that it is only natural that the development of revolutionary technologies and investments in them take decades to show up in the productivity of the overall economy.

That "diffusion lag" has been described by the economic historian Paul David, who used the electric dynamo as an example. Invented in 1866 by Werner von Siemens, the dynamo made possible the electrification of all kinds of production processes. Nevertheless, it showed up in American productivity statistics no earlier than the 1920s.[14]

Today's new technologies are adopted much faster than was the dynamo. But to implement them efficiently is an even greater challenge. "Computers are not dynamos," David writes. "The nature of man-machine interactions and the technical problems of designing efficient interfaces for humans and computers are enormously more

Figure 3.2
Information and Communication Technology Investment
in the United States, Germany, Italy, and France
(as a percentage of nonresidential
gross fixed capital formation)

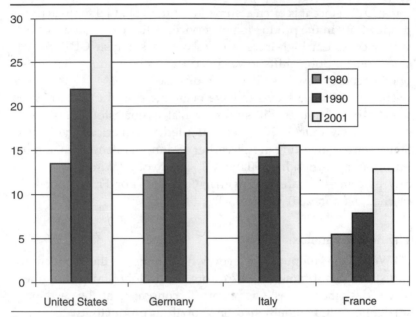

SOURCE: OECD (www.oecd.org).

subtle and complex than those that rose in the implementation of electric lighting and power technology."[15]

Despite that challenge, the ICT revolution has, in some ways at least, surpassed earlier technological revolutions. The British economic historian Nicholas Crafts, for instance, has calculated that the contribution of ICT to economic growth in the United States over the last 25 years "has exceeded that of steam and at least matched that of electricity over comparable periods."[16]

"The Solow productivity paradox stems largely from unrealistic expectations," Crafts concludes. "The true paradox is why more should have been expected of ICT."[17]

Just Another Bubble?

Of course, the uptick in productivity growth might have been just another bubble. With the end of the bull market and the economic expansion of the 1990s, the end of the productivity miracle may be near as well.

Increased productivity growth is indeed only natural in times of strong economic growth because fixed costs per unit decrease as production increases, causing overall unit costs to dwindle. Robert Gordon, the most prominent new economy skeptic among America's economists, estimates that as much as a third of the productivity growth in the late 1990s was cyclical in nature.[18]

But many indicators point to the fact that structural factors played a more important role than did cyclical factors:

- According to a study by the McKinsey Global Institute, only six sectors of the economy were responsible for 99 percent of the increased productivity growth between 1995 and 1999: retail, wholesale, securities, telecommunications, semiconductors, and computer manufacturing; together, they make up no more than 30 percent of U.S. economic output. And the productivity growth within those sectors can be further traced to activities of individual corporations. The McKinsey study attributes a whopping 23 percent of productivity growth in retail to Wal-Mart alone. Another 46 percent comes from competitors such as K-Mart who had to catch up in order to remain competitive.[19] Thus, productivity growth was very concentrated. Had it been a cyclical phenomenon, one would have expected it to be distributed more or less evenly throughout the entire economy.
- After a dip in 2001, labor productivity growth has picked up again. In 2002 it reached 4.9 percent—the highest annual increase since 1950. Although a productivity growth rate of more than 4 percent was also recorded in the first years after the recessions of 1974, 1982, and 1991, subsequent growth decreased significantly. In the current cycle, however, a far more favorable pattern becomes apparent. In 2003, the second year of economic recovery, productivity growth was very strong again at 4.5 percent.[20] Most experts see this as an indication that the strong productivity gains in the late 1990s were in fact mostly sustainable in nature.[21]

Indeed, high tech in the United States did not evaporate along with the hundreds of dying dot-coms. In 2003 more than 10 million people worked in ICT-related occupations. The revenues of Intel and

Sun Microsystems in 2002 were roughly four times the level they had reached as recently as 1995; meanwhile, revenues of Microsoft quadrupled, and Cisco Systems saw its revenues increase almost eightfold.[22] And there are also signals of further growth. Real gross private investment in information processing equipment and software in 2003 exceeded the record set in 2000 by more than 11 percent.[23]

Despite all the flops and failed business models, the dawn of the digital age in the economy surpasses in parts even the most optimistic estimates published at the height of the Internet hype. The technology-consulting firm Forrester Research predicted in 2000 that consumer online purchases would reach $52 billion in 2002. In the spring of 2003, another Forrester survey showed that revenues in 2002 actually amounted to $76 billion—almost 50 percent more than was predicted earlier.[24]

Why then, one may ask, did all those dot-coms go belly up? Why then the dramatic crash of the NASDAQ?

Turbulences, Setbacks, and Coincidences

Overreactions, optimistic and pessimistic alike, are a defining characteristic of technological revolutions. When the railroad—a revolutionary new mode of transportation—was introduced in the 19th century, it seemed for a while that the laws of gravity no longer applied to economic growth in the United States and Europe.

The optimism soon came to an end. Projects like the Northern Pacific Railroad in the United States turned out to be gigantic failures. Euphoria was followed by disillusion: investment levels plummeted overnight, and the entire economy was severely hampered. As important as railroads were for emerging industrialized economies, their advance was not steady; it was instead characterized by constant ups and downs.[25]

The history of ICT looks similar. Whenever the sector was in dire straits, another technological innovation came along that kindled a new dynamic. In the mid-1970s it was the creation of the personal computer, in the mid-1980s the combination of faster microchips, better software, and lower prices. In the early 1990s the creation of the World Wide Web followed.[26]

"We are indeed witnessing a revolution," Alvin Toffler, the prominent American futurologist, says. "But the last thing you will find in such a revolution is linear progress. The opposite is to be expected: turbulences, instability, setbacks, and many coincidences."[27]

Toffler points out that the first factory owners during the industrial revolution used their own families as laborers—much like they had done on their farms. But that, according to Toffler, didn't work out: "The elderly could not handle the fast speed of those machines and the children hated the work so much that they had to be chained to the machines. Something similar is happening today: We don't know which business models are the right ones in an information society."[28]

Furthermore, it is impossible to estimate how fast a new technology will be adopted by businesses and consumers. Had Internet traffic doubled every three and not every nine months, a lot more dot-com business plans would have succeeded; the extremely high stock market notations of many tech industries would have been justified.[29]

And the Winner Is . . . the Consumer

Given those uncertainties, rather extreme ups and downs on the stock markets are only to be expected. In times of rapid technological innovation, entire markets or at least segments thereof are likely to be over- or undervalued.[30]

In the case of the NASDAQ in the 1990s, an important misjudgment was added to the uncertainties: stockholders, brokers, and entrepreneurs alike assumed that profitability would increase along with productivity.

The assumption isn't far-fetched. In the previous 50 years, profits and productivity had been strongly correlated.[31] Not so during the boom of the 1990s. Despite rapid productivity growth, corporate profits as a share of GDP started to decline markedly in 1998—well before the end of the economic expansion (Figure 3.3).

The decline of profits was particularly pronounced in the ICT-producing industries. But ICT-using companies, too, were affected. That, in turn, can only mean that stockholders didn't benefit as much as did employees and consumers.[32]

Actually, it appears that both employees and consumers cashed in. And there are indications that in both cases increased competition was the cause. In the late 1990s, unlike earlier in the decade, wages and salaries no longer lagged behind the leaps in productivity. The

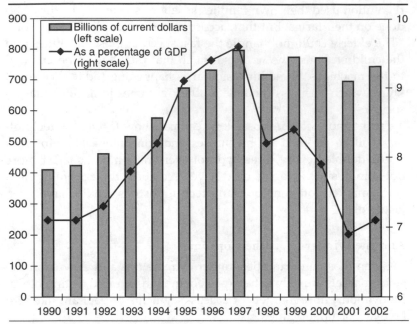

Figure 3.3
CORPORATE PROFITS IN THE UNITED STATES
(BEFORE TAX)

SOURCES: BEA (www.bea.gov) and author's calculations.

tight labor market undoubtedly had something to do with that since it handed more and more negotiating power to employees, leaving companies without control over their costs.[33]

In the long run, the consequences of ICT for corporate pricing power are probably even more important. It seems likely that many markets in a new economy will move toward the textbook description of perfect competition:[34]

- Markets become larger. For instance, bookstores that had a strong position in their local markets face competition from on-line stores such as Amazon.
- Markets become more transparent. Consumers can compare prices and services much more easily online before they buy cars, insurance, or airline tickets.

- Markets become easier to enter. In the offline world a new media outlet can enter the market only with a logistic exertion that usually only established publishers can afford. By comparison, the barriers to entry for an on-line newsletter are minimal.

Thus, competition tends to become more intense. Companies are forced to pass cost savings on to the consumer to a larger extent than they were in the past. By the same token, they have fewer opportunities to pass the burden of rising costs on to their customers. Consequently, profit margins dwindle.

Therefore, it is quite possible that the new economy turns out to be a curse for stockholders—but a boon to consumers. This, though, doesn't reduce the revolutionary force of those new technologies at all.[35]

Mostly Clear and Sunny

Whereto from here? Most U.S. economists have reduced their productivity growth predictions a little. But there is, nevertheless, widespread agreement that in the foreseeable future the productivity of the United States can achieve greater gains than were seen between 1974 and 1995.[36]

One should be cautious about such forecasts. After all, economists still can't explain convincingly what caused the slowdown of productivity growth in the 1970s. The productivity boom that started in 1996 also came as a surprise to most experts.

In addition, much depends on the speed of technological innovation. Of special importance, for instance, is the semiconductor industry's ability to continue to develop microchip generations every two years.[37]

It seems plausible, however, that at least over the medium term the new economy will deliver to Americans further high productivity growth:

- When new technologies are implemented, companies often suffer from disruptions of the production process. New kinds of work organization need to be developed; often, old and new technologies are used in parallel for a while; and workers need to be retrained. That, in turn, may well mean that productivity growth goes down at first. It is therefore possible that an increased level of high-tech investment has a depressing effect

39

on productivity growth in the beginning—to be followed by above-trend growth thereafter. In itself, this promises continuing rapid productivity growth for years to come.[38]

- Growth in the IT sector can snowball through the entire economy. The causes are two distinguishing features of information technologies: First, the development of IT products can cause high fixed costs. However, once a product has hit the market, it is cheap to serve one additional customer; the marginal costs are close to zero. The reason is that the consumption of (electronic) information, for instance software or databanks, is not rivalrous. Mr. A cannot wear a shoe worn by Mr. B at the same time. Software used by Ms. A, however, *can* be used simultaneously by Ms. B without the two of them interfering with each other. Second, many IT product markets display so-called network effects: The utility of a product increases with the number of its users. E-mail is conducive to information exchange only when enough people use it. Taken together, those two features imply that—unlike usual products—an increase in demand for IT does not result in higher prices. Instead, increased demand causes efficiency to increase and prices to fall. That in turn stimulates further increases in the amount demanded.[39]
- Computers are, as Robert Solow put it, everywhere. Initially, they performed difficult algorithms only. Later they were used for massive amounts of simple calculations. Finally, computer-based product design followed, as did industrial robots, warehouse management based on scanner data, and, of course, the Internet. An end of the IT boom would demand that at least one of two decades-old trends wither: either the advance in data-computation capacity would have to slow down or no new useful applications be found.[40]

The new economy and the productivity boom that rests on it are obviously very real phenomena. Both have, so far at any rate, survived the dot-com bubble's bust, a recession, and a stock market crash.

Therefore, the fate of individual ICT-producing companies shouldn't be confused with the fate of the industry itself. And dwindling profit margins and stock prices should not tempt us to underestimate the economic potential of these technologies.

A few questions, however, remain: Why has this potential only shown its face in the United States? Why is the share of ICT investment in Germany, France, and Italy so much lower than in the United States? And why is it that, to paraphrase Robert Solow, we see the computer age everywhere except in Europe's productivity statistics?

4. Europe's Sluggishness—A Chosen Lot

"Government is not the solution to our problem, it *is* the problem." That was a slogan Ronald Reagan used again and again during his 1980 campaign for the presidency. Like no other sentence, that quote represents a paradigm shift in the United States that was discernible from the mid-1970s on.

For the prior half century it had mostly been the market that was considered the problem. As they did in Europe, politicians in America drew the conclusion from the Great Depression that markets, for all their benefits, tend to cause crises, suffering, and injustice. It was up to the state to rectify that—with a strong hand or at least a solid grip.

Especially from the 1930s to the 1960s, the U.S. government expanded its encroachment on the economy. Beginning with Jimmy Carter (1977–81) and, much accelerated, under Ronald Reagan (1981–89) that trend was reversed. The American economic system underwent a sweeping liberalization:

- Taxes were lowered. In 1978 "Proposition 13" obligated California's local governments to lower taxes. The success of that proposition had nationwide reverberations. With the Reaganite tax reforms of 1981 and 1986, the top marginal rate of the federal income tax was lowered from 70 percent to 28 percent. The minds behind that reform were the so-called supply-siders, some of whom hoped that lower initial tax revenues would be more than made up for by higher economic growth. That hope was not realized. Budget deficits were at times during the mid-1980s more than 6 percent. But arguably that ensured that the second goal of supply-siders, seldom expressed explicitly, was achieved. The constant fear of holes in the budget reined in the spending frenzy of the U.S. Congress. Federal expenditures as a share of GDP went from 23.5 percent in 1983 to 21.8 percent in 1990. That share continued to sink throughout the 1990s and in 2000 reached its lowest point since 1966 at 18.4 percent.[1]

- Product markets were deregulated and public enterprises privatized. In 1978 the airlines and electricity were deregulated; in 1982 the AT&T monopoly was broken up; in 1987 Conrail went public in what was then the largest initial public stock offering in the nation's history.[2] Some of those measures, like breaking up AT&T, were carried out only half-heartedly. Other measures, such as partial deregulation of financial institutions, were flawed in their design.[3] Or they followed, as happened with electricity deregulation in California, not economic reason but the pressures of business and consumer lobbies. But it's clear that deregulation began earlier and was more thorough in the United States than in continental Europe. The share of GDP produced by extensively regulated sectors fell between 1977 and 1988 by almost two-thirds to 6.6 percent.[4]

- Welfare state regulations were reduced. From the 1980s onward, the minimum wage was only dilatorily adjusted to inflation. In 2001 dollars, the minimum wage stood at more than $6 at the end of the 1970s;[5] today it is $5.15. And the 1996 welfare reform put a five-year lifetime limit on welfare entitlement. The trend toward more and more welfare recipients—until then independent of economic conditions—was broken. In 1994, 14.2 million Americans received welfare payments; in June 2003 barely five million, the lowest number since 1967, did so.[6]

- The power of unions was diminished decisively. Ronald Reagan started that diminution by firing 11,000 striking air traffic controllers. As federal employees, the controllers were violating the no-strike clause of their employment contracts, which had not been enforced by Reagan's predecessors. Reagan's move was like a fire alarm. Private businesses also started making increasing use of their right to fire employees.[7] The number of states that guarantee workers the right to decide for themselves whether or not they want to join a union increased further.[8] Those factors helped to drive down decisively the share of the workforce that belonged to unions—from 20 percent in 1983 to 12.9 percent in 2003. Whereas 260 million workdays were lost because of strikes in the 1970s, the 1990s saw only 46 million workdays lost to strikes.[9]

France Ranks 123rd

Of course, there were trends in the other direction as well. After the Reagan tax reforms the maximum marginal tax rate was raised again to 31 percent by George Bush senior (1991) and by Bill Clinton to 39.6 percent (1993). Only the recent tax cuts by George W. Bush brought the top rate back down to 35 percent in 2003.

Along with all that deregulation and liberalization came a flood of new regulations, especially environmental, consumer protection, and labor law regulations.[10] In 2002 federal agencies issued 4,167 new regulations. Some economists estimate that the cost of federal regulations exceeds 8 percent of America's GDP.[11]

There can't be any doubt, though, that the United States has a far more liberal economic system than France, Germany, or Italy. In the 2003 edition of the *Economic Freedom of the World Report*, a survey prepared by the Canadian Fraser Institute in cooperation with the Cato Institute and many other research organizations around the world, the United States ranked third among countries with the greatest economic freedom—right after the city-states of Hong Kong and Singapore (Figure 4.1).

Germany, in contrast, ranked 20th. Italy ranked 35th, and France ranked 44th. That the European countries don't have worse rankings is partly due to the euro, which earns them favorable ratings for "Access to Sound Money"; Germany also ranks high in the categories "Freedom to Exchange with Foreigners" and "Legal Structures and Security of Property Rights."

When it comes to labor market regulations, however, Germany is ranked 80th of the 80 countries examined. Italy comes in 76th and France 41st whereas the United States is ranked third. Similarly depressing are the European countries' ratings for the size of their governments: Of 123 countries, Italy is ranked 96th, Germany 107th, and France 123rd; the United States is 22nd.[12]

The labor market and the size of the government are indeed the two aspects in which the American model arguably distinguishes itself most pointedly from its continental European counterparts:

- Employment protection legislation, for instance, is much stricter in France, Germany, and Italy than it is in the United States (see Chapter 20). And wages are determined in a much more centralized way. In Germany, for instance, collective wage agreements that unions and employers' associations agree upon are regularly imposed on businesses and hundreds of thousands, if not millions, of employees who weren't, even indirectly, represented in the negotiations—upon order by the government and without regard to the consequences for profits

45

Figure 4.1
Economic Freedom Ranking of the United States, France, Germany, and Italy

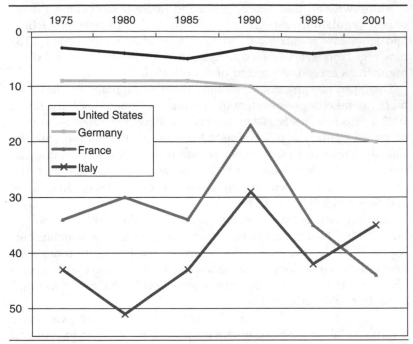

Source: Gwartney and Lawson (2003), pp. 78, 80, 96, 157.

and levels of employment. Thus, collective wage agreements de facto turn into cartel contracts. As a rule, there is no escape from such a cartel. According to German law, deviations from those contracts are legal only if they favor the employee. German courts have interpreted that as meaning that employees may not accept lower wages than the collective bargaining agreement prescribes, not even if that's the only way to save their jobs or the very existence of their company.[13]

- The American government has stayed relatively trim. According to the statistical definitions of the OECD, the U.S. government has never spent more than 38 percent of GDP. The respective record levels of Germany, France, and Italy are much higher (50, 55 and 58 percent). Currently, only Italy has a level

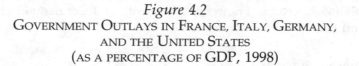

Figure 4.2
GOVERNMENT OUTLAYS IN FRANCE, ITALY, GERMANY,
AND THE UNITED STATES
(AS A PERCENTAGE OF GDP, 1998)

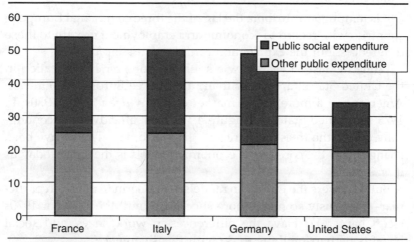

SOURCES: OECD (www.oecd.org) and author's calculations.

of government spending that is significantly below its record high. In 2003 government expenditures in the United States were 35.9 percent of GDP, in Italy 48.5 percent, in Germany 49.4 percent, and in France 54.4 percent.[14]

The transatlantic differences are mostly due to the higher level of social expenditures in the European countries. In 1998 those expenditures ranged from 25 to 29 percent of the respective GDPs—almost twice as high as in the United States (Figure 4.2). In all other kinds of expenses, taken together, the differences were relatively small. In Germany, for example, they were not even two percentage points above the American level.

On the revenue side, there is of course a dramatically higher tax burden in Europe. Consider, for instance, the difference between what employers pay out in wages and social security charges and what employees take home after tax and social security deductions. According to the OECD, that tax wedge on labor in the United States in 2003 amounted to 29.4 percent of total labor costs for a single production worker who had average earnings and no children; in

47

Italy (45.3 percent), France (48.3 percent), and Germany (50.2 percent) the wedge was far bigger.[15]

Innocent Suspects

It is tempting to attribute the lag of the three continental European countries with regard to economic and employment growth to those differences. But the explanation can't be that simple.

While the last 25 years saw a spurt in economic liberalization in the United States far greater than in the three European countries, America had a more liberal market economy even in the 1970s. In 1975 the United States, as Figure 4.1 shows, already was economically one of the freest countries in the world, too. There have been changes, but the core of the economic models is the same today as it was then.

But why were the European models—the German model in particular—obviously so much more successful until the 1960s or 1970s (see Chapter 1)? Have the differences in work, taxes, and social benefits perhaps nothing to do with the divergence?

Of course, that is entirely possible. But that would require the occurrence of so-called asymmetric shocks, economically relevant developments that affected one side positively or negatively but not the other.

One obvious shock was the introduction of the euro. Critics of the new European currency may argue with some validity that France, Germany, and Italy suffer from the restrictions of the stability pact. That pact, after all, allows members of the EU to run budget deficits of more than 3 percent only under exceptional circumstances. However, countries have only limited possibilities of stimulating a cyclically weak economy with aggressive fiscal policies.

In the case of Germany, which gave up the deutsche mark, it's further arguably true that the country entered the euro zone with an overvalued exchange rate and that it has now been suffering for years from short-term interest rates that are too high, given the state of its economy.

But the euro, for all its alleged downsides, has plenty of advantages as well, especially the elimination of exchange rate risks in transactions between the euro-zone countries. Therefore, what its overall effect is on balance is difficult to judge.

Another factor often mentioned as an excuse for Germany's performance is the reunification of the Federal Republic of Germany and the eastern German Democratic Republic. After all, year after year in the 1990s, West Germany transferred about 4 percent of its GDP eastward.[16] The result was a higher tax burden for the West German economy, which in turn depressed profit expectations and therefore companies' willingness to invest.

But the dragging effect of additional expenditures is, though substantial, hardly gigantic. According to estimates by experts of the European Commission, those expenditures have adversely affected Germany's economic growth by about .3 percent annually since the mid-1990s.[17] Annual growth in Germany was 1.3 percent on average between 1995 and 2003; the growth of the U.S. economy was an average 3.2 percent. Thus, the difference in growth rates was 1.9 percentage points, meaning that less than one-sixth of that difference was caused by reunification.[18]

What is worrisome is not so much the additional burden on the German economy, anyway. It is the fact that while East Germany has almost a third of its demand financed by the West, these billions seem to disappear without a trace.[19] All the investment in high-speed rail networks, highways, and state-of-the-art fiber optic networks failed to spark economic development in the East.

In every year between 1997 and 2002, East Germany grew slower than West Germany. That is to say, the divergence between the two parts of the country got bigger, not smaller. Indeed, in 1996 economic output per working-age person in the East stood at 61 percent of the West German level. In 2002 that number was down to 58 percent.[20] And a further decline seems likely. In 2003 the East German economy did slightly better than the West, but this is at least partly due to an even higher than usual amount of transfers from the West after a devastating flood in Eastern Germany in the summer of 2002; for the years 2004 and 2005, anyway, economists in early 2004 saw the East falling behind again.[21]

Thus, the situation becomes even more depressing if East Germany enters into German-American comparison (see Chapter 1). In principle, a resumption of the convergence process should have followed reunification. That is what the theory of diminishing returns as well as common sense would suggest. With a decrepit infrastructure, an underdeveloped service sector, and factories that made better museums than places of production, the former GDR obviously had a lot of catch-up potential. Therefore, a reunified Germany should have, starting from a lower level but boosted by especially high growth rates in East Germany, begun to catch up again with the United States. But that simply did not happen.

And no matter how much damage reunification and the euro did to economic growth, both "shocks" can hardly be blamed for the fact that the process of convergence between France, Germany, and Italy on the one hand and the United States on the other broke off more than 20 years ago. After all, reunification took place in 1990, and the euro was not introduced until 1999.

Indeed, empirical studies confirm that the sluggishness in countries like Germany and France is not the result of asymmetric shocks but a voluntarily chosen lot. A study by the International Monetary Fund, for instance, has shown that if only unemployment benefits, the taxation of labor, and employees' protection against dismissal were reduced to the American level, unemployment would decrease by more than three percentage points (Figure 4.3) and economic output could increase by 5 percent. The effect would double if product markets, too, were liberalized by as much as they have been in the United States.[22]

If those measures were undertaken, the prosperity gap vis-à-vis America could be reduced to about its 1980 level; unemployment could be brought to lows not seen for 20 years. And that doesn't take into account the positive growth and employment effects that could be expected if, for instance, time limits on welfare payments and the regulation of working hours and fixed-term contracts were cut back to U.S. levels, too.

However, two questions still remain: just why did Europe's version of capitalism work so well until the 1970s, and why has it only since then been surpassed by American cowboy capitalism in terms of growth and employment?

Resisting Structural Change

Germany is still a very industrial country. In 2002, 32.5 percent of the workforce were employed in the industrial sector (broadly defined as other than the agricultural and services sectors). At 32.1 percent, the Italian share was similarly high (Figure 4.4). Of the 30 member states of the OECD, only the Czech Republic, Hungary,

Figure 4.3
EFFECTS OF ECONOMIC "AMERICANIZATION" ON UNEMPLOYMENT RATES IN THE EURO ZONE
(EXPECTED DECLINE IN PERCENTAGE POINTS)

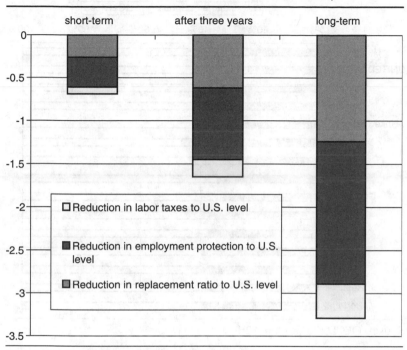

SOURCE: IMF (2003), p. 143.

Portugal, and the Slovak Republic had higher rates of industrialization. Is that a symbol of success, an indication that Germany's and Italy's factories are taking increased global competition in stride?

One might think so. A closer look, however, reveals a dismal picture. It's not the strong development in the industrial sector that explains the employment structure shown in Figure 4.4; rather, it's weak development of the service sector.

Generally economists agree that nations on their way to prosperity move through certain sectoral changes in employment structure. According to the "Three-Sector Hypothesis," in a poor country many people work in agriculture. With increased productivity, labor in this sector becomes redundant and is thus freed to work elsewhere—

Figure 4.4
EMPLOYMENT BY SECTOR IN SELECTED COUNTRIES
(2002, IN PECENT)

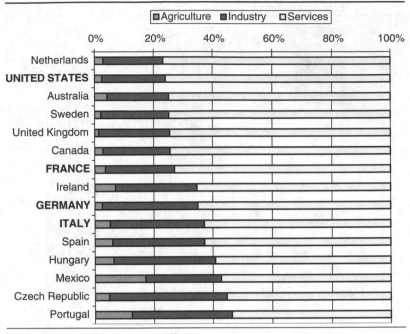

SOURCE: OECD (2003b), pp. 32ff.

the precondition for industrialization. At first, a continually decreasing portion of the population remains in agriculture while employment in the industrial sector increases. Growing productivity, finally, sets labor free in the industrial sector, too; this again is the precondition for the development of a modern service economy.

Figure 4.4 supports that theory. In relatively poor industrialized countries such as Mexico or Portugal, agriculture is significantly more important, while the most developed countries tend to have the largest service sectors. The Netherlands is at the top of that list—not surprisingly for a trading nation that has traditionally focused on services. The Dutch are followed by Anglo-Saxon and Nordic nations. Approximately three of every four employed people in those countries work in service industries.

In Italy and especially Germany, the share of employment in agriculture is, as can be expected, small. But that the size of the service sector in Germany (65 percent) and Italy (63 percent) is notably smaller than in, for instance, the United States, is not natural; indeed, it is alarming.

That's because highly developed economies can't expect employment miracles from their industrial sectors. Even a growing demand for industrial products can often be met with a constant or even shrinking workforce. The reason for that is the high potential for automatization and consequent growth of productivity in the industrial sector.

While the American service sector, for instance, created millions and millions of jobs, employment in the industrial sector actually declined by 3 percent between 1980 and 2002. In Italy and France, the decline amounted to 10 and 25 percent, respectively. Only in Germany, where reunification had led to a temporary 35 percent rise of employment in the industrial sector, was the number of jobs 1 percent higher in 2002 than it had been in 1980.[23]

One could assume that those numbers prove Jeremy Rifkin right (see Chapter 2). Indeed, if you look at the industrial sector alone, the "end-of-work" prophets aren't far off the mark. "The factory of the future," an economists' joke has it, "has just one man and one dog. The man's job is to feed the dog. The dog's job is to keep the man from touching the equipment." But even so, Rifkin and friends aren't correct. The simple reason is the endless potential for job creation that the service sector offers.

Service-sector jobs are often and gleefully defamed. Service jobs, it is said, are for the most part mundane, low-paying "McJobs." However, the opposite is true, as 1998 numbers for OECD countries show. For every 100 jobs for low-skill workers, manufacturing provided 97 jobs for medium- or high-skill workers. The service sector provided jobs for 229 medium- and high-skill workers for every 100 low-skill jobs. In producer services, the ratio was even more impressive at 100 to 417. What is more, 19.4 percent of the service-sector workers had a university education; in manufacturing the share was just 8.2 percent.[24]

Every so often, it is also said that even a modern economy needs a strong industrial base because the service sector produces nothing tangible and therefore can't be the foundation of an economy. Even

Adam Smith, the otherwise sharp spiritual grandfather of capitalism, thought so. Only industrial work, wrote the Scottish philosopher in 1776, can be "productive." The work of a service provider, however, "adds to the value of nothing."

Why Smith erred can be shown with an example. In the past, almost everyone who worked *for* the agricultural sector also worked *in* agriculture. In today's modern economies, only a few percent of workers are employed *in* agriculture. But many service providers work *for* this sector—for example, software engineers who write the programs that help farmers manage their business or scientists who develop genetically modified seeds.

Thus, as an economy matures, employment tends to shift from the actual production of goods toward jobs that, broadly speaking, help to make the production process more efficient. That's one of the reasons why a large share of services jobs in the employment structure is typical of highly developed economies. Therefore, strong growth in service-sector jobs is a sign that the structural change that is necessary to make the transition to a service-sector economy is functioning. That's what's so unsettling about Figure 4.4; Germany and Italy are obviously lagging far behind.

What's more, the gap is especially pronounced in business services, financial services, and other knowledge-intensive services—in those areas of the service sector, in other words, that offer a disproportionately high share of well-paying jobs. In five such knowledge-intensive service industries, real output in the United States grew by no less than 195 percent between 1980 and 2003 (Figure 4.5).

The continental European countries also experienced growth in those industries, but considerably less than America. In Germany and Italy, the increase amounted to 118 percent and 140 percent, respectively. In France, growth was limited to 103 percent. (That indicates that the rather high employment share of the service sector in France does not actually reflect an encouraging pattern; rather, it seems that low-value services have a relatively great weight in the French service sector.)

Creative Destruction

The transition of industrialized countries into service societies, so-called tertiarization, is a quasi-natural process. However, the last

Figure 4.5
PRODUCTION OF KNOWLEDGE-INTENSIVE SERVICE INDUSTRIES IN THE UNITED STATES, FRANCE, GERMANY, AND ITALY
(BUSINESS SERVICES, COMMUNICATION SERVICES, EDUCATIONAL SERVICES, EQUIPMENT LEASING, FINANCIAL INSTITUTIONS, HEALTH SERVICES, TRILLIONS OF 1977 DOLLARS)

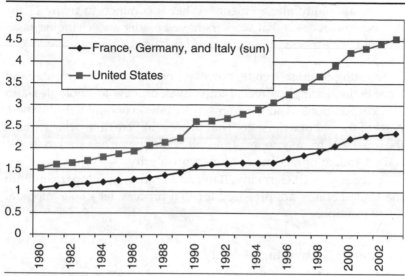

SOURCE: Global Insight.

decades also witnessed developments that were neither natural nor even predictable:

- Globalization: The reduction of trade barriers and falling transport and communication costs increase competitive pressures. Manufacturers in highly developed economies face more and more competition from emerging markets and developing countries.
- The faster pace of technological progress: The revolution in information and communication technologies itself drives structural changes. However, it also facilitates innovation in other sectors such as the pharmaceutical industry.[25]
- The move away from "Taylorism": According to the theory of Frederick Winslow Taylor, which was adhered to by executives in the United States for decades, the employee of a corporation

55

is a link in a chain that has only to perform exactly a set of dictated tasks—no less but no more either. The realization that efficiency is improved when employees are motivated and, along with management, actually do some thinking only became consensus when in the 1970s Japanese corporations began to conquer world markets with the help of more modern methods such as "total quality management." What is common to many of the new practices is that workers have broader and changing tasks and are expected to accept more responsibilities.[26]

Adapting to those trends, however, necessitates that capital and labor be increasingly directed into new jobs, new technologies, and new corporations. And in order for the new economy to be created, parts of the old one must go. That process of "creative destruction," the great Austrian economist Joseph Schumpeter has shown, is the central source of increasing human prosperity.

To see how well Germany, Italy, and France, in comparison with the United States, are prepared for that process, let's take a look at a few examples.

Example 1: Geographic Mobility

When established industries in a region go under, the only thing that can prevent a permanent rise in unemployment is structural change. Either fresh capital flows into the region—attracted for example because the lower demand for labor has put downward pressure on wages—or the unemployed move away.[27]

That process of adapting to new realities obviously functions more smoothly in the United States than it does in Europe. For instance, in Germany, a country the size of Montana, just 1.44 percent of the population in 2001 moved from one state to another. In the United States, on the other hand, the number of inhabitants moving into another state was on average 2.65 percent annually during the 1990s, that is, more than 80 percent higher than in Germany.[28]

In America, the groups that are often hit hardest by unemployment, especially low-income earners and young people, move to wherever the jobs are rather than wait for the jobs to move to them. More than 4 percent of low-income earners moved to other states annually in the 1990s. In booming cities such as Atlanta, Austin,

Denver, Phoenix, and San Francisco, the number of 20- to 24-year-olds in the population grew by more than 50 percent during the 1990s; in Las Vegas it almost doubled. In old industrial cities such as Buffalo, Cleveland, and Pittsburgh, on the other hand, the number of young adults went down drastically.[29]

This high degree of mobility likely did much to balance regional differences in unemployment. Indeed, in December 2003 the difference between the state with the lowest unemployment rate and the one with the highest was, seasonally adjusted, just 4.4 percentage points. In 43 of the 50 states the unemployment rate was within a rather narrow range of 2.5 percentage points (between 4.0 and 6.5 percent).[30]

The situation in Germany, however, was quite different: In the Western German states in December 2003, the range was 6.6 percentage points; in Germany as a whole, it reached 13.7 points. In all of Europe, the differences are larger still. Despite the introduction of the right to move freely inside the European Union more than a decade ago, unemployment in the EU in 2001 varied between 2 percent (Berkshire, England) and almost 25 percent (Calabria, Italy).[31]

Example 2: Education

Especially in the Anglo-Saxon world, Germany was long envied for its highly structured system of vocational training that brought forth a wide base of well-qualified and specialized industrial workers and craftsmen. Germany's universities, too, produce relatively highly specialized human capital.

In comparison, education in America tends to be rather more conceptual than skill-specific.[32] To require that bouncers prove in an examination their "wide-ranging qualifications before taking up their profession"—as the German state of Northrhine Westphalia does—is rather un-American, to say the least.[33] In that sense, Klaus Zwickel, a former prominent German union leader, was actually quite right when he claimed a few years ago that Germans have "professions" while Americans have "jobs."[34]

In the industrial age, the German educational model helped to make "made in Germany" a trademark synonymous with quality, and it contributed to the strong gains in productivity that made possible continuous wage and salary increases in the postwar decades.

Also, it seemed logical to support this system with strict employment protection legislation and rather generous unemployment benefits. After all, those who are highly specialized must expect relatively large and long-lasting losses of income when they become unemployed.[35]

But what if technological progress picks up speed and constantly demands new skills? What if the modern organization of production processes increasingly demands flexibility? Then, of course, a worker who enjoyed a conceptual rather than a skill-specific education has the edge—a worker whose education taught her how to learn rather than just assemble facts and formulas, a worker who has rather general skills and therefore can be employed in many jobs and trades and who is, precisely because of that, less in need of being shielded from income losses by strict employment protection laws and high unemployment benefits.[36]

Example 3: Bankruptcies

Every bankruptcy is a story of pain, especially for the employees who lose their jobs. Preventing bankruptcies through state interventions, however, can be counterproductive even from the employees' perspective. A prime example is the case of Philipp Holzmann. When this large German construction company was about to go under in the fall of 1999, its workers called for help from the Berlin government. And why not? Which employee doesn't want to keep his job? Who wants to move to a different city or learn completely new skills in order to prevent unemployment?

Still, Chancellor Schröder's willingness to save those jobs with federal loan guarantees would have been questionable even under normal circumstances. With or without Holzmann, the same number of streets, bridges, and office buildings would have been built in Germany and the same number of people would have been employed in construction—because all that depends, not on the number of construction companies on the market, but on demand.

What made the Holzmann episode particularly absurd is that the German construction industry suffers from large overcapacities. That means that this industry will lose jobs one way or the other; the only question is, where? The intervention of the chancellor, thus, meant only that instead of employees of Holzmann (which in the end went into insolvency in 2002 anyway), other construction companies' employees lost their jobs—employees of companies that were smaller, more efficient, and could possibly have survived.

The Holzmann case exemplifies that, when bankruptcy reflects structural adjustments to changes in demand or technologies, a high number of bankruptcies can actually be a good sign. In those cases bankruptcy is an indication of structural change that is working.

The disappearance of unproductive companies from the market is indeed one of the four potential channels through which labor productivity growth can be generated. The productivity of an economy increases

- when existing companies increase their efficiency,
- when market shares shift from relatively unproductive to more productive companies,
- when start-up companies are more productive than established ones, and
- when companies with less-than-average productivity disappear.

With regard to both market entry and market exit, the dynamism is much greater in the United States than in Germany. In West Germany, between 1989 and 1994, 735 of every 10,000 private businesses left the market annually. In the United States, an annual 1,012 per 10,000 companies went out of business. A comparison of start-ups looks similar. For every 10,000 companies, West Germany had 906 start-ups annually; in the United States the number was 1,240.[37]

The lower rate of market entry in Germany is hardly surprising. After all, it is much more burdensome to found a company in continental Europe than it is in the United States. One study, for instance, looked at what government regulations cost an entrepreneur in terms of time and money to set up a new enterprise. An American entrepreneur setting up a new business faces a one-time regulatory cost that amounts to 1.7 percent of the annual U.S. per capita income. In Germany the corresponding number is 32.5 percent. In France and Italy it is even higher at 35.6 and 44.8 percent, respectively.[38] Those numbers represent significant barriers to establishing new business enterprises.

Those differences are likely to be one of the reasons why, when the sources of productivity growth are studied, a completely different picture emerges for the United States than for the European nations. In manufacturing, the exit of firms in the United States between 1992

Figure 4.6
DECOMPOSITION OF LABOR PRODUCTIVITY GROWTH IN THE
UNITED STATES, ITALY, FRANCE, AND GERMANY
(MANUFACTURING; PERCENTAGE SHARE OF TOTAL ANNUAL
PRODUCTIVITY GROWTH)

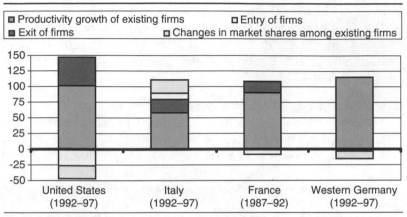

SOURCES: OECD; and Scarpetta, Hemmings, Tressel, and Wee (2002), p. 40.

and 1997 contributed almost 46 percent to the growth of productivity (Figure 4.6).[39] The contribution of market entry of new firms was significant also but negative (a possible reason is that whenever a great number of start-ups hit the market, productivity growth is slowed because the newcomers are small at first and cannot realize economies of scale).[40]

In France and Italy, on the other hand, most of the gains in productivity can be attributed to efficiency gains within existing firms; in Germany they were the sole source of productivity growth.

Insolvencies, by contrast, played a far smaller role in the European countries than in America. In Germany, they even made a negative contribution to productivity growth. This is an indication not only that relatively few companies exit the market in Germany but that those that do are often the wrong ones. There seem to be, in other words, many Holzmanns in Germany.

Example 4: High Tech

The new economy lives—but not yet in France, Germany, or Italy. As argued in Chapter 3, the revolution in information and communication technologies has not led to higher productivity growth there so far.

One of the reasons is that the ICT industries themselves are smaller than in the United States. The three European countries have few global players in this field. A look at the "Info Tech 100," a ranking in which *Business Week* lists the 100 most important IT companies worldwide, confirms that. As of March 2004, 44 of those companies were from the United States; 4 were from France; only 1 was from Germany, and only 1 was from Italy.[41]

The Europeans have fallen behind not only in information and communications technologies but also in cutting-edge research and high-tech production in general. According to whichever indicator you prefer—total research and development expenditures, R&D expenditures per capita, or research efforts as a percentage of GDP—Americans are spending much more than the French, Germans, and Italians (Table 4.1). The number of researchers relative to the size of the workforce is also higher in the United States, as is America's market share in the production of Nobel laureates. Thus, it is not surprising that growth in the production of high-tech goods has been greater by far in America than in France, Germany, and Italy.

So while the United States managed to maintain its leading position in the production of high-tech goods in comparison with emerging Asia, continental Europe is slowly being removed from the major league. Since 1997, for instance, the output of high-tech goods has been higher in tiny Singapore than in Italy. On a per capita basis, it was more than three times higher in Korea in 2003 than it was in Germany.[42]

No wonder even Germany's Federal Ministry for Education and Research comes to dismal conclusions. In a 2003 report the ministry noted:

> Germany loses, if not quite as drastically as Japan, ground on international technology markets. Germany's comparative advantages in the production of research-intensive goods have further declined in the 1990s. This continues a trend which started in the 80s. . . . In the 90s, it turned out that the German export-portfolio has become increasingly "car-heavy." If one were to, for argument's sake, exclude the car industry from the trade statistics, Germany could no longer be considered a country that in international trade is specialized on research-intensive production.[43]

Table 4.1
Research and High-Tech Production in the United States,
France, Germany, and Italy

	United States	France	Germany	Italy
1. Gross domestic expenditure on R&D, 2002, PPP adjusted[a]				
Billions of dollars	277.1	36.1	55.1	15.5
Per capita	964	591	668	268
As a percentage of GDP	2.67	2.20	2.51	1.07
2. Researchers[b]				
Number in thousands[c]	1,261	177	264	66
Per thousand of total employment	8.6	7.2	6.8	2.9
3. Nobel laureates, 1990–2003, share in percent[d]				
Chemistry	69.0	0	3.4	0
Medicine, physiology	71.0	0	9.7	0
Physics	76.5	8.8	0	0
Economics	88.5	0	3.8	0
4. Production of high-tech goods, 2003[e]				
Output, billions of 1997 dollars	912.2	176.6	124.2	42.1
Real growth since 1980, in percent	+419	+242	+52	+69

Sources: Global Insight; Nobel committee (www.nobel.se); OECD (2004), pp. 18ff; and author's calculations.

[a] Italy: 2000.
[b] USA: 1999; Italy: 2000; France and Germany: 2001.
[c] Full-time equivalents.
[d] Categorization based on country of residence at the time of the award.
[e] Computer and office equipment, communication technologies, pharmaceuticals, air and space technologies.

Obviously, a lack of creative destruction—in Germany at least—ties down capital and labor in companies and industries that produce mature technologies and therefore have little potential for growth.

However, also of importance is why German (and French, and Italian) *users* invest far less in information and communication technologies and why their ICT use does not show up in macroeconomic productivity statistics.

A company's productivity increases, not simply with the purchase of new technologies, but rather with their efficient use. Often that demands changes in production processes or whole company structures. That was already the case when electrification was introduced. That technological invention led to the replacement of multistory factories located in city centers by single-story factories that needed more room and were thus built outside the cities.[44]

Today things are similar. ICT, too, have brought productivity gains to only those companies and industries that coupled investment with sweeping organizational restructuring.[45] Whether such changes are even possible, however, depends, of course, on the regulatory frameworks companies face.

As pointed out in Chapter 3, a significant portion of the productivity gains of the American economy in the 1990s can be traced back to increases in efficiency in retail. With the help of massive use of information technologies, companies such as Wal-Mart and Home Depot optimized their logistics, lowered their inventory stock, and began to track their customers' purchasing patterns.

That, however, becomes really worthwhile only when economies of scale can be realized. In the United States they can be. Restrictions on shopping hours are minimal. Furthermore, building codes are relatively lax, allowing retailers to build so-called big boxes. Home Depot stores in the United States, for instance, are as large as 165,000 square feet.[46]

In Europe, by contrast, retailers find it much harder to realize economies of scale; that is the key reason why not even Wal-Mart can make it in Germany. The retail giant's expansion onto the German market was stalled when it found it impossible to apply the same business strategies that had made it so successful on its domestic market.[47]

Labor market regulations also play an important role. With the use of new technologies, some jobs become obsolete while others are created. The easier it is for employers to fire or at least move employees, the more quickly the return on ICT investments will show up. On the other hand, all-too-strict employment protection legislation can prevent ICT investment from occurring in the first place. Why, after all, introduce new technologies that make it possible to reduce the payroll when reducing the payroll is a very costly, if not impossible, venture?[48] (That point will be addressed again in Chapter 16.)

Eurosclerosis—20 Years Later

The examples make it obvious that the big continental European economies are not well equipped to adapt quickly to new and constantly changing environments. Rigidities that are caused by government regulations or institutional arrangements, such as Germany's combination of skill-specific education and strict employment protection legislation, may once have caused little disruption or even on balance provided benefits. In times of increased pressure for economies to adjust, however, they seem to be an impediment.

It is therefore not so much the "Rhineland" model per se that is the problem as its inflexibility in times when flexibility is key. It is rather unable to absorb negative shocks and use positive shocks effectively.

That insight is anything but new. As early as in the early 1980s Herbert Giersch warned about "Eurosclerosis." With that term, the long-time president of the Kiel Institute for World Economics expressed his concern about the "institutional rigidities and structural constraints that are an inherent part of Rhineland capitalism." Those rigidities and constraints, Giersch argued, are unsuitable for the "age of Schumpeter" that he farsightedly saw dawning.[49]

Several empirical studies indeed show that it was mostly the superior adaptability of America's "cowboy capitalism" that explained the much more desirable trends in employment in the United States in the 1980s and 1990s. One of those studies, for instance, shows that between 1970 and 1995 the flexibility of the U.S. labor market alone was responsible for at least half the divergence between the unemployment rates in the United States and other industrial countries.[50]

Of course, structural change doesn't happen without any impediment in the United States, either. Bailing out big companies isn't unknown in America. Just think of Chrysler or the integrated steel mills. Still, it's clear that companies in the United States—less restricted by government regulations but also less protected—went to work earlier and more radically adapted to the changing economic environment.[51]

How large a role creative destruction played in that restructuring process can be shown by comparing the German and American stock markets.

Of the 20 publicly listed companies in the United States with the highest market capitalization in 1967, only 11 were still in the top 60 at the beginning of 2004. Prominent companies such as Kodak, Polaroid, and Xerox were no longer even in the top 60, but many companies that didn't even exist 35 years ago were: Amgen, Dell, Home Depot, Intel, Microsoft, and Oracle, to name just a few.[52]

Only one of the 20 German companies that had the highest market capitalization in 1967 has gone under since then. No fewer than 15, on the other hand, still made the top 20 in 2002. And the remaining 4 were all still in the top 60.[53]

5. America's Golden '90s—Was It All Just Hype?

Unemployment and inflation in America fell and then fell further. The federal government ran a budget surplus and the stock market climbed from historical high to historical high. Even the emerging market crisis that started in 1997 could not weaken the economy's performance.

The expansion of the U.S. economy that began in March 1991 was an unprecedented boom. It lasted 10 years to the month—longer than any other expansion since records were first kept in 1854. Between 1995 and 2001, the United States contributed 63 percent to global economic growth; Europe, in comparison, contributed only 8 percent.[1]

Then, rather abruptly, it was all over. The success stories of recently celebrated companies turned out to be pies in the sky—or just plain lies. Long-time investors' favorites, such as stocks of high-tech companies, fell dramatically, sometimes with no end in sight. High-rolling freely spending companies suddenly scrapped their investments. The federal deficit came roaring back again. Unemployment rose; between February 2001 and June 2003, the United States saw a loss of 2.6 million jobs. And although inflation continued to be low, it was so low at times that there was fear of deflation.[2]

Was the euphoric mood that went along with the boom of the 1990s all just hype inflated by the media, stock market analysts, and politicians?

Unpaid Bills

The recession began in March 2001 and ended eight months later, in November. It was one of the mildest as well as one of the shortest of the last 30 years.[3] But the lack of dynamism that the American economy has displayed since the recession is worrisome. In 2002 GDP grew by 2.2 percent. In 2003, the growth rate picked up to 3.1 percent, which is about the pace that most economists now consider the U.S. economy's long-term potential.[4] In the early stages of a cyclical recovery, however, economies usually achieve above-trend growth.

It's to be expected that the recovery after a mild recession will be weak at first. Strong growth rates that are often observed when an economy is beginning to pick up again are typically the result of consumption and investment bouncing back from very depressed levels. In the recession of 2001, though, private consumption, which makes up roughly 70 percent of the economy's demand, continued to grow. That it afterwards increased at a slower pace than it did after previous recessions is therefore only natural.

Still, by historical standards, the upswing in 2002 and 2003 looked disappointing. What's more, even those rather low growth rates were largely achieved by aggressive economic policies. Historically low interest rates were a huge boost to the economy. In June 2003 the Federal Reserve lowered its federal funds target rate to 1 percent, the lowest level since 1958. Fiscal policy loosened up, too. Increased government spending was responsible for 31 percent of total output growth in 2002 and 20 percent in 2003.[5]

Even more significant in the medium term seems to be the fact that the 2001 recession, unlike earlier slowdowns, has done very little to remove America's economic imbalances, the most important of which is usually considered the current account deficit. Actually, the current account deficit, after declining slightly in 2001, continued to grow larger.

Put simply, a current account deficit occurs when a nation consumes and invests more than it produces—and therefore needs to borrow money from abroad. In America that is the case. In 2003 the current account deficit reached a record high of almost $542 billion.[6] That is equal to almost $1.5 billion per day—and close to three times the amount of private net capital flows into emerging countries.[7]

Current account deficits get corrected. The consequence is usually that the growth of economic output lags behind its long-term potential for about three to four years. For industrialized countries, such a correction typically sets in when the deficit reaches 5 percent of GDP; in 2003 the U.S. current account deficit stood at 4.9 percent.[8]

There is another problem: although the U.S. current account deficit financed private investment in the late 1990s, it now serves for the most part to pay for growing budget deficits. The difference is important since investment outlays for, say, IT, tend to boost potential output. A deficit put to such use can, under certain circumstances, be sustainable for a rather long time. After all, as debt rises, so does the debtor's ability to pay it off.

The situation looks different when, as is now the case, the current account deficit stems from plugging holes in the federal budget. Money spent on tanks creates short-term demand, but it does not increase the growth potential of an economy. Money spent on security measures at airports or monitoring container ports may well even lower that growth potential.[9]

The End of the Dividend

The fall of communism in Eastern Europe did not cause the boom in the United States, but it certainly fueled it. The end of the Cold War allowed for a drastic reduction in military expenditures. From a share of 6.2 percent of GDP in 1986, defense spending fell to 3.0 percent in 1999–2001,[10] an essential prerequisite for the federal budget to run surpluses starting in 1998.

That "peace dividend" was possibly the second (after the revolution in information and communication technologies) most important positive economic shock of the 1990s: The smaller the budget deficit, the smaller the government's demand on capital markets. That leads to less private demand being crowded out; interest rates that corporations pay for their investment spending and households for their mortgages and consumer credits decline.

Empirical evidence suggests that that effect is considerable. A study by Federal Reserve economist Thomas Laubach, for instance, shows that long-term interest rates fall by a quarter point when the expected budget deficit drops one percentage point in relation to GDP.[11] The reduction of the deficit in the late 1990s could, therefore, have lowered interest rates by anywhere from 100 to 200 basis points—an enormous stimulus for a modern economy.

With September 11 came the turnaround. The Bush administration's original plan to follow Ronald Reagan in using tax cuts to enforce spending discipline (see Chapter 4) was defunct. In real terms, government consumption and investment expenditures were 10.2 percent higher in 2003 than they had been in 2000. A large part of the story is the increased Pentagon budget. According to government estimates as of early 2004, national defense spending will, on average, amount to 3.8 percent of GDP in fiscal years 2003 through 2005.[12] Add to that rapidly rising increases in public expenditures for homeland security.

That growth in government spending—rather than lower revenues due to tax cuts, the stock market slump, and the economic slowdown—is the main cause of the roaring deficits. If, for instance, revenues had been the same as they were, while federal spending had grown by only 2 percent annually between 2000 and 2003, the budget deficit in 2003 would have been $116 billion, less than a third of the actual $375 billion budget deficit. Keeping nominal spending constant would have led to a deficit of no more than $7 billion in 2003.[13]

Whatever their cause, large budget deficits will sooner or later likely mean rising real long-term interest rates. That alone will probably hamper private investment—and may over time affect productivity growth and thus the U.S. economy's dynamism.

The long-term prospects for the U.S. economy are further diminished by demographic aging. Today, every sixth American is over 60 years old; in 2040, every fourth will be. That will put the Social Security system under enormous strain. Either future employees and their employers will face spiraling payroll taxes, or retirees will get only a fraction of what they are being promised today.

Reforms are urgently needed because the baby boomers will start to retire in large numbers within a couple of years. That's a trap from which it will be difficult to escape: every year the number of contributors to the system will shrink by a large increment while the number of recipients will grow by the same large increment.

European Conditions?

Large deficits and demographic aging are likely to dampen America's future economic growth. It would therefore be rather surprising if the U.S. economy were to grow for years on end by rates of over 4 percent, as it did in the 1990s. The 1990s may well be remembered by Americans as the good ol' days.

But that hardly means that America is facing European conditions. First, if put into international perspective, the public sector in the United States does not look that heavily indebted. To be sure, in the past the situation of public sectors in countries such as France and

Figure 5.1
GOVERNMENT DEBT IN THE UNITED STATES, FRANCE,
GERMANY, AND ITALY
(GENERAL GOVERNMENT GROSS FINANCIAL LIABILITIES AS A
PERCENTAGE OF GDP)

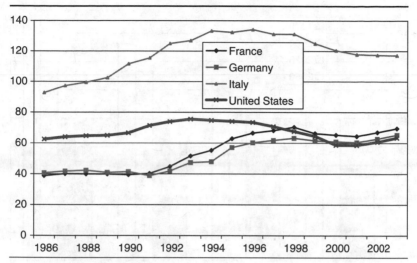

SOURCE: OECD (2003), Annex Table 33.

Germany looked more favorable than that of the United States (Figure 5.1). But while U.S. general (federal, state, and local) government gross liabilities as a percentage of GDP are still below the levels they reached in the late 1980s, they have increased by more than half in France and Germany. Thus, in 2003 liabilities were lower in the United States (63.4 percent of GDP) than in Germany (65.3 percent) and France (69.5 percent). And if anything, the situation in the United States is better than it seems because Figure 5.1 does not reflect that government employee pensions in the United States are partly funded—whereas in France and Germany they are not.

Second, aging in France, Germany, and Italy will be far more pronounced because fertility rates are lower and fewer immigrants are allowed to enter (Figure 5.2).

On top of that, today's employees in Europe, unlike employees in the United States, are being promised that they will receive much more than just a basic income when they are old. So the explosion

71

Figure 5.2
AGING IN THE UNITED STATES, FRANCE, GERMANY, AND ITALY
(PEOPLE 60 YEARS OLD AND OVER
AS A PERCENTAGE OF TOTAL POPULATION)

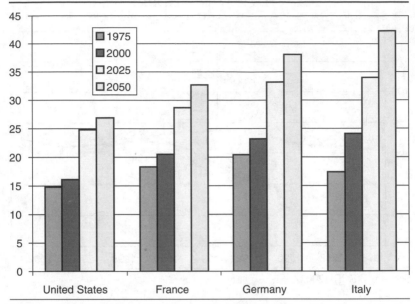

SOURCES: United Nations (2002), pp. 232, 244, 282, 462; and author's calculations.

of costs in Europe will be accordingly higher. Simply cutting entitlements drastically will probably not be a politically feasible option for European governments because seniors are highly dependent on public pensions. In 2000, for instance, just 35 percent of the after-tax income of American households headed by over-60-year-olds consisted of public benefits. In France, Germany, and Italy the share was 67, 61, and 59 percent, respectively. For the middle fifth of the income scale, the share of retirement income that came from public benefits was 54 percent in the United States but between 78 and 84 percent in the three European countries.[14]

Here to Stay

Looking forward, the picture for the United States looks far brighter than for the continental European countries. Looking backward, the same is true. With regard to both productivity and employment, the United States made gains that are very real, that are here to stay, and that countries such as France, Germany, and Italy were simply unable to realize.

Without the acceleration of productivity growth since 1996, America's GDP would have been roughly 10 percent lower than it was in 2003. That shot in the arm of American prosperity would not disappear even if the U.S. economy should, starting tomorrow, return to the low productivity growth rates experienced between 1974 and 1995.

The same is true for the labor market: Unemployment in the United States reached over 6 percent in the summer of 2003—a level that Italy, Germany, and Italy don't even reach anymore under the best of economic circumstances. And as dismal as the labor market might have looked in the early stages of the most recent economic upturn, that does not undo the past spur in employment. After all, during the 1980s and 1990s, the number of employed people grew by 1.9 million—annually.

Or, to look at it from a different angle: One would be justified in calling talk about America's job machine "hype" if the slowdown after the 1990s boom had erased so many jobs that longer-run employment growth were no better than in comparable countries. However, that is clearly not the case. Take, for instance, the number of employed people as a measure: Labor market performance since 1991 would look as depressing in the United States as it does in France, Germany, and Italy only if 14.5 million fewer people had been employed in 2003.[15]

6. A Misery Desperately Longing for Justification

France, Germany, and Italy lag behind the United States, no matter which economic component you look at. Take per capita income, employment, productivity trends—comparison does not bode well for the three largest continental European economies. However, perhaps statistics don't give the complete picture.

Europeans certainly are richer than official statistics would indicate. There is no doubt that the disparity of living standards in Europe and the United States is smaller than America's significantly higher per capita income would suggest.[1] One reason is that the shadow economy in Europe is larger than in the United States. According to calculations by Friedrich Schneider, a German economist and leading international authority in this discipline, the French underground economy reached 14.8 percent of official GDP in 2002–03. In Germany it amounted to 16.3 percent; in Italy the figure was a staggering 26.2 percent. In the United States, on the other hand, it stood at a relatively meager 8.6 percent.[2]

Nature is another part of the equation. America experiences more extreme weather than continental Europe with its moderate climate. A more substantial part of U.S. economic output is therefore put toward the prevention and repair of damage caused by natural disasters such as hurricanes and tornadoes. And higher expenditures for energy are in part explained by the more extreme temperature differences in the United States and the consequent greater consumption of heating fuel and electricity for air conditioners.

Americans also spend more money on fighting crime. Since the mid-1970s the number of prison inmates has risen dramatically. At the end of 1980 half a million people were incarcerated. By now, that number is way over two million. No other country in the world has that high a proportion of its population behind bars.[3] (The consequences for the labor market are discussed in Chapter 13.)

In 2001 America spent $57 billion on prisons and jails alone. Upkeep of the police and the courts cost another $72 billion and $38 billion, respectively. Per capita, that came out to more than $580.[4] Furthermore, there are indirect costs. Those include, for example, the loss of output that is incurred by locking up citizens who could otherwise do a lot of work.

Furthermore, households and businesses spend more on security than they do in Europe. Take, as an example, the four million Americans who live in gated communities; in Houston the share of people living in such neighborhoods has already reached 22 percent.[5]

The comparatively higher expenses of fighting crime and the whims of nature mean that Americans have less money available for other purposes. The difference between the living standards in Europe and the United States is therefore smaller than a look at per capita incomes might lead one to believe.

Can't Buy Me Love

The statistics in the previous chapters are misleading in other ways as well. They don't account for everything that really matters; and not everything that is counted matters really.

Calculations of per capita income are based on gross domestic products. Simplistically put, the GDP represents the market value of all goods and services produced in one year—neither more nor less. Housekeeping chores performed by a cleaning lady or a nanny enter the statistics; a homemaker's work, however, does not surface in the GDP.

Politicians, then, should have their eye on more than just the GDP and per capita income. Thus, Gerhard Schröder got it right when he said, "For us, quality of life is more than just standard of living, more than consumption or income levels."[6] Quality of life, for instance, increases when—thanks to medical advances—life expectancy does. Furthermore, money or GDP numbers do not make happiness. Sounds like a cliché, but empirical studies have shown that relationships are more important for individual well-being than mere money.[7] For the calculation of GDP, however, neither life expectancy nor personal relationships have import.

All that matters here because not only are the material living standards in Europe, relatively speaking, higher than a comparison of per capita income suggests; quality of life is also higher than a comparison of material living standards suggests.

As discussed in Chapters 3 and 4, a good proportion of growth in employment and productivity in the United States can be attributed to the trend toward large supermarkets, warehouses, and malls usually located in suburbia. That trend not only promotes efficiency in retail, thereby helping to make consumer goods more affordable; it also makes life easier for the consumer, at least if frequent shopping is considered a chore.

But the increase in efficiency takes its toll on another aspect of the quality of life. Retail businesses in inner cities are struggling with competition from suburban outlets. Strolling through downtown areas, leisurely promenading on boulevards—so popular in Europe—is for the most part a thing of the past in the United States.[8]

As regrettable as that may be for Americans, it can hardly justify the meager employment and growth rates of countries such as France, Germany, and Italy. Even if U.S. bureaucracies and lawmakers had been able to stymie the growth of Wal-Mart, Home Depot, and so forth with Euro-style regulatory laws and building codes, the United States would still have far outpaced the European countries in terms of growth and employment over the last 25 years (see Chapter 10).

Leisure Time vs. Overtime

Why not have a little more free time instead of a higher income? Well, perhaps because the price paid for it is higher than it seems at first. That is so since not only the employee takes a pass on wage or salary. At the same time less income can be taxed; that is, the tax base shrinks. Consequently, transfer payments and other expenditures must be cut or higher tax rates must try to make up for the loss in tax revenue. Because that, in turn, weakens work incentives, additional negative growth effects may occur that go well beyond the immediate repercussions of reducing the workload.

Still, it isn't necessarily a bad sign when a third of the working-age population (as in Germany) or even close to half of it (as in Italy) is not employed. Nor is it necessarily a positive thing that a larger and growing percentage of the population works in the United States. Theoretically, that could be attributable to the fact that more and more women find themselves forced to work in order to make up for the decreased purchasing power of their spouses' income (an assumption, however, that turns out to be wrong in the case of the United States, as will be shown in Chapter 11).

Therefore, how the large transatlantic differences in employment levels are to be judged is in the last instance dependent on the extent to which they occur voluntarily. Surely, unemployment in continental Europe is not solely the result of voluntary decisions. That would seem a very bold assumption in countries such as Germany where six million people are openly and hiddenly unemployed. But there *are* voluntary elements, to be sure. Otherwise the right to enjoy six weeks of vacation per year wouldn't be treated as something like a basic human right in Germany's economic policy debate whereas many Americans have to content themselves with half or less.

Precise estimates, however, are impossible to make. Northwestern University economist Robert Gordon, for instance, estimates that the difference in employment levels is one-third voluntary in nature but calls the number "a wild guess."[9]

Whether it actually is a third or a tenth or half, it is obvious that quality of living in Europe and the United States converges further when leisure time is taken into consideration.

Growth vs. Justice

Adjusted for price level differences, per capita income in the United States exceeded the French level by about 36 percent in 2003. At 42 and 44 percent, respectively, Germany and Italy lagged even further behind.[10] Those differences are so pronounced that, even after taking account of the higher crime- and climate-related expenses, it is safe to say that the material standard of living is higher in the United States.

The difference in living standards, in turn, seems to be so big that it would be daring to claim that the continental European countries provide a better quality of life—even after taking account of downtown strolling and more free time. Given the continued transatlantic divergence of per capita incomes, it can further be assumed that that gap is bound to become wider.

What's more, the above-mentioned caveats only state that the same per capita income would result in a higher standard of living and quality of life in continental Europe. Those caveats don't change a thing about the United States' ability to produce a higher income per capita in the first place.

However, two aspects that may more than compensate for all U.S. advantages, economic justice and security, have not been examined. Per capita income is a simple average. But such averages are of only limited use. Just how limited is easily shown with a comparison of Hungary and Saudi Arabia. Both countries have roughly the same per capita income. But infant mortality in Saudi Arabia is triple that in Hungary. Hungary has an illiteracy rate of 1 percent; in Saudi Arabia a sixth of men and every third woman can't read and write.[11]

Applied to the European-American comparison: Does America's impressive lead in per capita income perhaps hide the fact that incomes and wealth are distributed in a way that is incompatible with a well-defined idea of justice and fairness? Has a larger part of the American population not profited from the increase in economic output? In America, do the rich get richer and the poor stay poor? Can countries such as Germany or France claim to produce a more just society for which it is well worth accepting inferior economic growth and employment rates?

What's more, "[q]uality of life has," as Chancellor Gerhard Schröder puts it, "much to do with freedom, freedom from fear and misery, that is."[12] Undoubtedly many people want safety: safety especially from having to accept unwanted cuts in their attained quality of life. Do Americans have a higher quality of life but one that's always uncertain and under threat? Do the European economies provide a lower but more certain quality of life free from the fear of unemployment and poverty?

Part III of this book will discuss economic justice and security in more detail. But first, Part II will take a closer look at the stereotypes about America that are so popular in Europe.

PART II

THE UNITED STATES: MYTHS, HALF-TRUTHS, AND REALITY

7. "Living Standards Are Declining"

For Americans, it just gets worse and worse. At least, that's what you hear after each recession. After the one that ended in 1991, for instance, Princeton economist Paul Krugman wrote about the "age of diminished expectations." And there was talk that Generation X would be the first cohort in America's modern history that had to expect a lower standard of living than its parent generation.

The indicator that pessimists most enjoy pointing to is the trend of hourly wages. It does indeed look disheartening. The average hourly wage of production and nonsupervisory workers in the private sector increased significantly in the 1950s and 1960s. Since the 1970s, however, it has been decreasing in real terms (Figure 7.1). Only during the boom of the 1990s did it gain ground again. Measured in current dollars, the average approached $15.50 in late 2003. Accounting for inflation, however, it still was about 8 percent below the peak it reached in 1973.

But looking only at hourly wages is misleading:

- Hourly wages reflect earnings before taxes. The tax burden, however, has decreased significantly since the 1970s. Therefore, disposable income has grown significantly faster than changes in gross income would indicate.
- Health insurance and other voluntary employers' benefits play an increasing role in compensation. According to a 2003 survey by the U.S. Chamber of Commerce, 372 employers paid, on average, 21 cents in voluntary medical, retirement, and savings benefits for every dollar paid in wages or salary.[1]
- An ever-larger share of household income is earned not through work but as dividends, capital gains, and interest. In 2001 about 52 percent of U.S. households owned stock directly or indirectly through pension and mutual funds. Even among households in the lowest fifth of the income scale, the share was at 12.4 percent. In Germany the share of stockholders over 14 years of age was 20 percent.[2]

83

Figure 7.1
Hourly Wages in the United States
(EARNINGS OF PRODUCTION OR NONSUPERVISORY WORKERS ON
PRIVATE NONFARM PAYROLLS, JANUARY OF EACH YEAR,
SEASONALLY ADJUSTED)

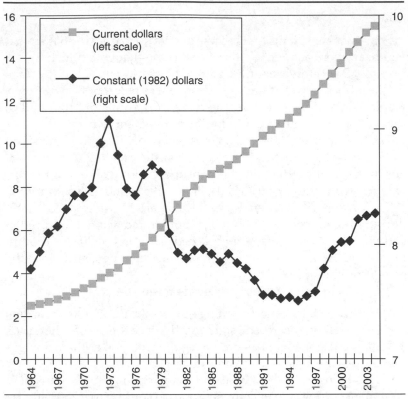

Source: BLS (www.bls.gov).

Add to this the fact that Americans work more than they used to. More women work and more people work full-time rather than part-time jobs (see Chapter 2). To gauge the standard of living of the average U.S. family, it therefore makes more sense to look at overall *household* incomes.

Wages vs. Income

A common indicator American statisticians use to measure household income is "money income," which includes, among other

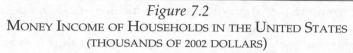

Figure 7.2
MONEY INCOME OF HOUSEHOLDS IN THE UNITED STATES
(THOUSANDS OF 2002 DOLLARS)

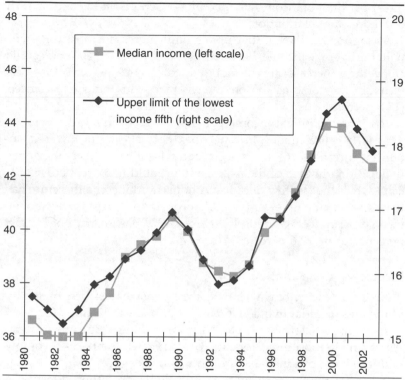

SOURCE: U.S. Census Bureau (2003), pp. 17, 25.

things, earnings, unemployment compensation, Social Security payments, interest, dividends, and rents.[3]

A look at the trend of money incomes in real terms since 1980 shows that the income of the average household suffered setbacks during the recessions of the early 1980s and 1990s from which it would not recover for years (Figure 7.2). Those setbacks, however, were finally more than offset by strong gains in the following economic upswings. Overall, there is a clear upward trend.[4]

A rising average could of course hide the fact that low-income earners were excluded from the positive development. But that this isn't the case becomes clear when we look at the 20th percentile of

85

the income range. The 20th percentile includes those households that earn less than the 80 percent of households with the highest earnings but more than the bottom 19 percent. It thus also marks the upper limit of income attained by households in the bottom fifth of the income distribution.

As Figure 7.2 shows, that upper limit increased mostly in sync with the average income. Between 1980 and 2002, the 20th percentile enjoyed an increase in real money income (14.7 percent) that was virtually the same as the one an average household experienced (15.8 percent).

The increase in real income per capita was even more favorable. That is because money income does not reflect the lowered tax burden, increased voluntary social benefits, or realized capital gains. In addition, the size of the average household has declined significantly over the last few decades. A household income therefore has to be shared among fewer people. Accordingly, the *per capita* money income of an average household since 1980 has grown not by 15.8 percent but by 22.6 percent.[5]

Income vs. Consumption

Neither income nor wages are comprehensive measures of quality of life and material living standards. But other indicators, too, support the impression that is gained from looking at income growth. According to most indicators, the United States compares favorably with the large continental European countries (Table 7.1).

It is true for instance that, as the media on either side of the Atlantic do not tire of pointing out, the life expectancy of newborns is lower in the United States than in France, Germany, and Italy. What is hardly ever mentioned, however, is that, with increasing age, U.S. life expectancy catches up with and surpasses life expectancy in other countries. A 50-year-old American has a higher life expectancy than a German of the same age.

A look at the Human Development Index (HDI) further brightens the picture for the United States. The HDI includes life expectancy and other measures of the quality of life and is meant to provide an alternative to per capita income as an indicator in international comparisons.

According to the 2003 HDI, Americans have the seventh highest quality of life worldwide. All other large industrialized nations are

Table 7.1
INDICATORS FOR LIVING STANDARDS AND QUALITY OF LIFE IN FRANCE, GERMANY, ITALY, AND THE UNITED STATES

	United States	France	Germany	Italy
1. Human Development Index				
Rank, 2003 report	7	17	18	21
2. Life expectancy				
Of a newborn boy, 2000	73.9	75.2	74.4	76.0
Of a 30-year-old man, 2000	45.7	46.8	45.7	47.3
Of a 50-year-old man, 2000	27.7	28.9	27.2	28.7
Of a 70-year-old man, 2000	12.8	13.8	12.1	13.1
3. Housing				
Average size of dwellings, square feet[a]	1,763	948	941	N/A
Homeownership rate, in %[b]	68.3	54.7	40.5	67.4
4. Consumer goods				
Ownership/users per 1,000 inhabitants				
Phone lines, 2001	665	573	635	474
Cell phones, 2001	444	605	683	846
Personal computers, 2001	623	337	336	196
Internet access, 2001	500	264	364	276
Ownership in % of households				
Freezer, 2001	99.8	N/A	99.3	N/A
Dish washer, 2001	53.0	N/A	51.3	N/A
Microwave oven, 2001	86.1	N/A	58.2	N/A
Clothes washer, 2001	78.6	N/A	95.1	N/A
Clothes dryer, 2001	73.6	N/A	33.3	N/A
Television, 2000	98.2	N/A	95.9	N/A
VCR, 2000	85.1	N/A	65.9	N/A
Cable television, 2000	68.0	N/A	54.2	N/A

SOURCES: Statistisches Bundesamt (2002), p. 544; Statistisches Bundesamt (2002a), pp. 26–27; United Nations Development Programme (2003), p. 237; United Nations Economic Commission for Europe (www.unece.org); U.S. Census Bureau (2002), pp. 605, 699; U.S. Census Bureau (www.census.gov); World Health Organization (www.who.int/en); and author's calulations.

[a]Useful floor space: U.S., 1997; France, 1996; Germany, 1998.
[b]U.S., 2003; France, 1999; Germany, 1998; Italy, 1991.

Table 7.2
PURCHASING POWER OF AVERAGE-WAGE EARNERS IN
THE UNITED STATES
(MINUTES OF WORK NEEDED TO AFFORD SELECTED CONSUMER GOODS)

	January 1980	January 2004	Change 1980–2004
Bread, whole wheat, per lb	6.5	5.3*	−18%
Whole frozen turkey, per lb	8.7	4.2	−52%
Bananas, per lb	2.9	2.0	−31%
Sugar, white, per lb	2.5	1.7	−32%
Coffee, 100%, ground roast, per lb	29.3	11.2	−62%
Electricity, per kWh	.48	.35	−27%
Gasoline, unleaded regular, per gallon	10.3	6.2	−40%

SOURCE: BLS (www.bls.gov), U.S. Census Bureau (www.census.gov), and author's calculations.

*October 2003.

behind: Japan ranks 9th, the UK and France rank 13th and 17th, respectively; Germany is 18th, and Italy is 21st.

Meanwhile, use and ownership of durable consumer goods are on a steady rise in American households. As Table 7.1 shows, for most product groups it reaches a higher level than in Germany.

Even America's low-income earners are fairly well equipped: 56.8 percent in the lowest income quintile have at least one car, 40.6 percent own their own home.[6] Indeed, homeownership among this group is as high as homeownership in Germany overall.

In any case, consumption has increased by more than income numbers might indicate. That is because the prices of many products that virtually every household buys to meet its basic needs were lagging behind overall inflation. For instance, an American employee who earned the average hourly wage of production and nonsupervisory workers in January 1980 needed to work 8.7 minutes in order to be able to afford one pound of a whole frozen turkey. In January 2004, 4.2 minutes sufficed (Table 7.2).[7]

In some cases, such as bread or turkey, increased productivity might have been the key reason that prices were held back. In others, such as electricity, the deregulation of markets is likely to have been an important factor. And for bananas or coffee, for instance, the dismantling of trade barriers may have helped.

Those developments mean that a household needs a smaller portion of its income than in the past to buy a basket of basic consumer products. This, in turn, frees money for other things, such as luxury goods (see also Chapter 8).

In the end, we can argue about how the development of living standards in the United States over the last quarter century is to be judged. If compared to the impressive 1950s and 1960s, the 1980s and 1990s might look disappointing. But whether John Doe's standard of living has continued to increase over the last 25 years is not open to question. It has.

8. "For Everything Else, There's MasterCard"

Europeans only shrug their shoulders when they hear how Americans have turned into a "credit card nation," as the title of a book has it. In February 2004, U.S. commercial banks had $264 billion in outstanding credit card debt on their balance sheets. Among nonhomeowners in America, such high-interest loans made up 40 percent of all debt in the 1990s.[1]

The stereotypes are all correct. Yes, Americans are highly indebted. Yes, easy access to credit cards, aggressive marketing by their issuers, and high interest rates may have contributed to financially trapping many Americans. And yes, Americans save little.

But are American families really *that* unwilling to save, as is often maintained? Is the standard of living a debt-financed phenomenon? Is even, as the German press would have it, "the prosperity in the United States *for the most part* debt financed"?[2]

Those Misleading Savings Rates

At the meetings of the finance ministers of the seven largest industrialized countries (G7), it has become a ritual to hand out a communiqué that offers each of the participants some advice.

On those occasions, the U.S. secretary of the Treasury regularly gets a reminder to encourage Americans to save more. In fact, the "old problem with the savings rate," as Germany's finance minister Hans Eichel has put it,[3] is tackled with such perennial routine that no one questions anymore how big the problem is or even if it actually exists.

After all, the statistics speak a clear language. Or so it seems. In relation to disposable income, personal savings in the United States averaged slightly more than 9 percent in the 1980s. In 2003 the rate was only 2 percent; earlier, in October 2001, it had even reached a record low of .6 percent.[4]

However, the savings rate is, as Federal Reserve economists Richard Peach and Charles Steindel point out, "a very distorted measure."[5] When government statisticians, for instance, calculate disposable income, they subtract capital gains tax payments from gross income; the capital gains themselves, however, are not taken into account. However, during the boom of the stock market in the 1990s, capital gains became a significant portion of income. And if incomes were greater than measured, then savings, too, must have been larger than indicated by the official savings rate.

Of course, a large part of those capital gains existed only on paper. And much of those savings was lost when the bubble finally burst. But even if only realized capital gains are taken into account, the savings rate in 1999 would have been seven percentage points above the official numbers. Savings would hence have been only marginally below the long-term average.[6]

In Debt—So What?

Nominally, outstanding household debt has more than tripled over the last 15 years. At the end of 2003 it reached a staggering $9.4 trillion—a sum greater than the government's debt of $5.6 trillion.[7] Growing debt, however, isn't necessarily a problem. Far more important is whether or not the ability to pay off debt and interest is impeded. In other words, what matters is how outstanding debt and debt service obligations relate to income and wealth.

In relation to disposable income, the debt of American households grew from about 60 percent in the 1970s to 90 percent in 2000. But the growth of wealth outpaced the growth of debt. The average American family as well as low- and high-income earners increased its net worth by more than 50 percent between 1989 and 2001 (Figure 8.1)—a fact hardly compatible with the claim that U.S. prosperity is "for the most part" debt financed.[8]

The international comparison in Figure 8.2 points in the same direction. The data presented suffer from limited comparability.[9] However, what seems to be clear is that households in France and especially Italy are financially on a footing that is slightly more solid than they are in the United States. The situation of German households, on the other hand, is apparently worse than that of their American counterparts. The bottom line at any rate is that the relation of property and debt in America is not particularly poor.

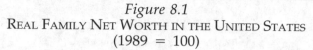

Figure 8.1
REAL FAMILY NET WORTH IN THE UNITED STATES
(1989 = 100)

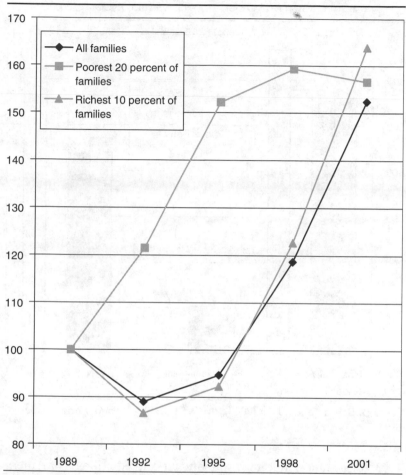

SOURCES: Federal Reserve Board (www.federalreserve.gov) and author's calculations.

Interest, Not Rent

The picture looks even better if debt service, rather than total debt, is considered. Debt service, certainly, is the more relevant factor when assessing the sustainability of the financial position of a household—and is not always in sync with total debt. Between 2001 and

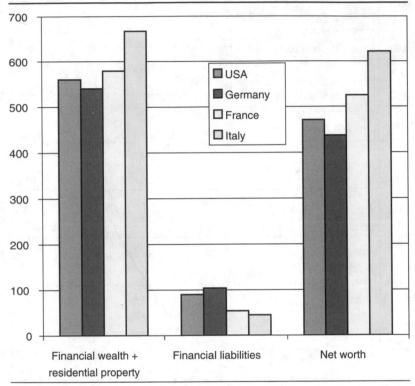

Figure 8.2
ASSETS AND LIABILITIES OF HOUSEHOLDS IN THE UNITED STATES,
GERMANY, FRANCE, AND ITALY
(AS A PERCENTAGE OF GROSS DISPOSABLE INCOME, 2000)

SOURCES: Babeau and Sbano (2003), pp. 9, 21, 23, 27, 29; and author's calculations.

2003, for instance, mortgage refinancing offered millions of Americans the opportunity to gain access to new capital while reducing their monthly payments. In other words, their debt grew but their debt service obligations were reduced. Refinancing also was used to pay down more expensive, non-tax-deductible consumer debt—in which case total debt might remain the same.[10]

Still, the debt service of American households grew modestly over the last years, according to official statistics. Outstanding mortgage and consumer credit debt, taken together, stood at 13.1 percent of income in the third quarter of 2003; 10 years earlier, the share was 10.9 percent.[11]

That trend needn't be troublesome though, as long as it doesn't accelerate too much. That's because, with rising incomes, the part of its income that a household must spend to satisfy its basic needs becomes smaller. In 1960 American households spent 29.9 percent of their disposable income on food, clothing, and shoes. By 1980 expenses for those kinds of necessities were down to 23.1 percent of disposable income; in 2003 the share was a mere 16.7 percent.[12] That means that more money is available for other things—luxury goods, for instance, or, yes, debt repayments.

Furthermore, rising debt service obligations also reflect the trend to homeownership. In 1990 fewer than 64 percent of households held property; by 2003 homeownership had increased to a historical high of 68.3 percent—even as the population grew considerably (see Chapter 7).

The homeownership boom allowed rental payments to decline from 3.5 percent of disposable income in 1990 to 3.3 percent in 2003.[13] That change might look minute, but it isn't when you consider the soaring housing prices during that time. However, unlike mortgages, rent payments are not considered part of debt. Therefore, official debt statistics show the increase in mortgage obligations but do not reflect the savings from a decrease in rent payments.

The Credit Card Nation

Looking only at the big picture, it is possible to miss important details. The moderate trend of growing debt may well hide a worsening financial situation for many households. A result of that would be an increasing number of households unable to service their debt. But, if you take into account cyclical fluctuations, that's not the case.

More and more households have been filing for bankruptcy since the Bankruptcy Reform Act of 1979 made it easier to do so. In 1980 fewer than 300,000 households filed for bankruptcy; in 2003 the number was close to 1.6 million.[14] Delinquency rates on consumer installment debt, however, haven't displayed any longer-term upward trend since 1980. Defaults on home mortgages have even trended downward significantly for more than 20 years. Neither of those trends has been ended by the latest recession.[15]

One possible reason is that the number of indebted households has been growing. That means that while total household debt increases, the burden *per* household might actually be getting smaller. Taking that effect into account, the mortgage burden indeed is at its long-term average. Official statistics for 2002 and 2003, on the other hand, have it at the highest level since 1988.[16]

The same goes for measures of consumer credit that include leasing contracts and credit card debt. Since the beginning of the 1990s consumers' cash and check purchases have fallen from about 80 to roughly 60 percent of all transactions; credit card payments make up most of the remainder. As with mortgage payments, more people seemingly share the burden of credit card debt.[17]

In addition, the growing popularity of credit cards itself creates more debt. That stems from the fact that credit card payments, as opposed to debit card transactions, are not immediately withdrawn from a bank account but are instead settled by the consumer at the end of a monthly period. So credit card owners constantly take short-term loans that show up in the statistics—even though little or no interest has to be paid for them when the invoices are paid immediately and in full.

Built on Sand?

Many Americans will likely have to content themselves with more moderate increases in consumption. First, as long as the stock market fails to provide capital gains of the magnitude that were realized in the 1990s, the savings rate of American households, as measured officially, will have to increase in order to keep effective savings at its long-term average. Economists at Goldman Sachs, for instance, estimate that the savings rate will have to grow to 6 to 10 percent of disposable income.[18]

Furthermore, many households will have to restrain their desire to consume in order to avoid a debt crisis. Mere stabilization of the interest rates means that the growth of debt must decrease if debt service obligations are not to increase.

That in the future the *growth* rate of the living standards might be lower than in the past, however, is still a long way from saying that the *level* they have reached is not sustainable. The typical American household is, after all, still far from ruin. As Federal Reserve chairman Alan Greenspan put it in early 2004: "Overall, the household sector seems to be in good shape, and much of the apparent increase in the household sector's debt ratios over the past decade reflects factors that do not suggest increasing household financial stress."[19]

Also, it usually takes extremely bad economic conditions to force consumers to cut back their spending. Between 1948 and 2003, real economic output contracted in 34 quarters; real consumer spending, on the other hand, declined in only 18 quarters.[20]

Thus, the prosperity American households enjoy might grow more slowly in the years to come. But the level attained today is simply not built on sand.

9. "Poverty Is on the Rise"

"And his hunger burns. . . ." Ever since Elvis Presley hit the radio waves with "In the Ghetto," Europeans have had the image of many Americans permanently excluded from riches. Unable to participate in the growth of wealth, the stereotype has it, an underclass populates inner cities in which conditions resemble those of Third World countries.

Perhaps this picture isn't completely untrue. The question, though, is: How pervasive is the problem? Is it getting better or worse? What are its causes? And is cowboy capitalism or something else to blame?

The Average Portuguese Isn't Poor—Or Is He?

In Europe poverty is usually defined in relative terms. Not just those who have too little to cover their basic needs are considered poor; everyone whose income lags behind the average is. The usual benchmark is the median income, that is, the level of income that is reached or surpassed by 50 percent of all households. More specifically, you are considered poor if the income of your household is less than half the median. According to that definition, the United States suffers from widespread poverty, indeed. At 17 percent, it is at any rate higher than in Germany (7.5 percent), France (8 percent), or Italy (14 percent).[1]

However, that criterion isn't really a measure of poverty, it's a measure of disparity. The reason is simple enough: As the median income climbs, so does the poverty line. Today, a German family with an income at the thus defined poverty line has about the same real income that an average German family did in the mid-1960s.[2]

International comparisons add another problem. Let's assume conservatively that the median income in the United States, adjusted to purchasing power parities (PPP), is only 30 percent higher than in Germany.[3] In that case, for households that earn between 50 and 65 percent of the German median income, poverty becomes a matter of geography: If they live in the United States, they are considered poor; if they live in Germany, they are not.

Or, to use a different example: The median household in Portugal has a PPP-adjusted income that is close to the poverty line in the United States. Nevertheless, no one would seriously claim that every second Portuguese household lives in poverty.[4]

Such comparisons suggest that one should use absolute rather than relative terms when looking at how many people have to live with an income that is not sufficient to cover their basic needs.

Rising Tides and Lifted Boats.

The United States has had such a measure for absolute poverty since the 1960s. Simplistically put, a family is considered poor when it does not earn more than three times the amount that a typical household of its kind spends on food.

The poverty line is then adjusted for inflation, using the consumer price index. Accordingly, anyone living at the threshold of poverty today has the same real income as a person with a poverty-line income 10, 20, or 30 years ago.

The number of poor according to that parameter has indeed increased significantly—from 23.0 million in 1973 to 39.3 million in 1993. By 2000 it had decreased to 31.6 million, but two years later it had risen again to 34.6 million.[5]

To assess a country's success in fighting poverty, it is, however, more important to look at the poverty rate, that is, the number of the poor relative to the population. In the United States, that number declined dramatically during the 1960s. Between 1959 and 1973, a mere 14 years, it was halved from 22.4 to 11.1 percent (Figure 9.1). Most experts at the time thought John F. Kennedy had been proven right. Kennedy had claimed that strong economic growth was the best way to combat poverty: "A rising tide lifts all boats."

After 1973, however, there are no clear indications of a causal relationship between economic growth and the poverty rate. In both 1983 and 1993 the share of people living in poverty reached more than 15 percent again.

Only in the most recent economic boom was the correlation between economic growth and poverty discernible. At the height of the expansion, in 2000, the poverty rate fell to 11.3 percent. That was the first time that it came close to the record low reached in 1973.[6]

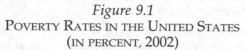

Figure 9.1
POVERTY RATES IN THE UNITED STATES
(IN PERCENT, 2002)

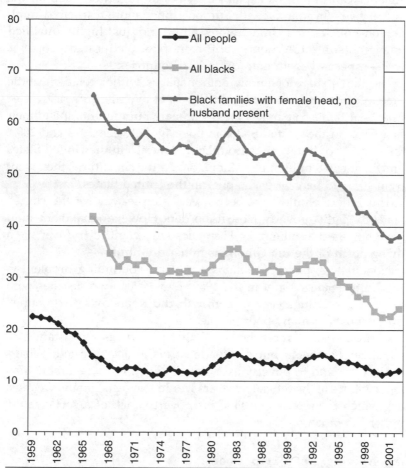

SOURCE: U.S. Census Bureau (2003a), pp. 22–25.
NOTE: No data available for missing years.

"Ghettoization," on the rise in the 1970s and 1980s, also diminished in the 1990s. The number of whites in high-poverty neighborhoods sank by 29 percent to 1.9 million while the number of African Americans in high-poverty neighborhoods dropped by 36 percent to 3.1 million.[7]

Immigrant Poverty

The number of poor people and the level of the poverty rate in America can in part be explained by the immigration boom of the last 30 years. In contrast with Europe's much more restrictive immigration policies, the United States allows not just highly qualified immigrants into the country but many poorly educated people as well—especially from Latin American countries.

The lion's share of immigrants manages within relatively little time to catch up with the income levels of average Americans (see Chapter 19). It's true nonetheless that many immigrants spend their first years in the United States in poverty. Between 1973 and 2002, the number of immigrants from Latin America in the United States grew from 10.8 million to 39.2 million. At the same time, they went from 10 to 25 percent of the poor in the United States.[8]

Thus, there would have been a very simple way for the United States to "fight" poverty: close its borders. However, that that would have helped the millions of Hispanics who want to try to make a living north of the Rio Grande is rather doubtful.

Nonetheless, poverty remains a big and continuing problem in the United States. Only in the 1960s and 1990s, two decades with extraordinarily high economic growth, did Kennedy's "rising tide" lift the boats of many poor people.

A closer look reveals, however, that poverty is a constant as a social phenomenon, but not for most *individuals* affected. What's more, the trend in poverty over time is much more favorable than a first glance at the official numbers would suggest. Finally, we must ask which is more responsible for poverty, lack of a social safety net or too much of it?

A Revolving, Not a Trap, Door

The risk of becoming poor and staying so can only be assessed if the fate of individuals or households is followed for a while in longitudinal studies. The only relatively recent official study of that sort was produced by the U.S. Census Bureau.[9]

According to that study, no fewer than 30.3 percent of the American population fell beneath the poverty line for at least two consecutive months between October 1992 and December 1995. Apparently, a large part of the population is exposed to the risk of poverty.

Looked at from that angle, the official poverty rate understates the problem.[10]

At the same time, the study showed:[11]

- Almost every second household that slipped into poverty for two consecutive months managed to escape it again within the next two months. After a year, three of four households had moved back above the poverty line.
- Only 5.3 percent of those whose income was beneath the poverty line at any time in 1994 were in that predicament for the entire 24 months of 1993 and 1994.

Thus, for most of those affected, poverty is only a temporary state, not a permanent fate. Poverty in the United States, to use the words of the study's author, turns out to be "a trap door for a few and a revolving door for many."

Short phases of income-poverty, however, can be bridged relatively easily, by either tapping into savings or taking out loans. Low-income households in the United States indeed consume a lot more than their income would suggest. For every dollar of net income, the income-poorest fifth of households spent $2.29 in 2002 (see Chapter 15).[12]

Out of Touch with the Real World

The calculation of the official poverty rate has long been criticized. According to scholar Nicholas Eberstadt, it nowadays depicts "a society with no recognizable correspondence to real-world America."[13] One point of criticism is that poverty is measured against a nation-wide average of consumer prices. That doesn't take into consideration the often dramatic differences in price levels across regions— and that many poor people live in regions with especially low price levels, such as areas near the Mexican border in Arizona, New Mexico, and Texas.

Furthermore, the calculation of the poverty line is based on a shopping cart full of goods and services that reflect the consumption habits of the average consumer. That the poor spend a particularly high percentage of their income on clothing, for instance, is not considered.

The consumer price index, moreover, does not reflect the actual development of the cost of living precisely. A committee of experts known as the "Boskin Commission" has placed the discrepancy at one percentage point per year. If that were correct, it would mean that people living at the threshold of poverty now have a purchasing power that is 35 percent higher than in 1973. A look at the households in question supports that notion. Be it a washer or a fridge, a TV set or an air conditioner, today's poor are better equipped with many durable consumer goods than average households were in the early 1970s.[14]

An even more important critique refers to the criterion used for the calculation of income. While cash transfers like unemployment benefits and welfare payments are included, transfers in kind are not.[15] That distorts the level of the actual economic position of poor families because cash transfers were reduced over the last decades while transfers in kind rose significantly:[16]

- Between 1960 and 1973 alone, overall welfare payments more than quadrupled in real terms. In the following two decades, they decreased despite a rising number of recipients. That is, the payment per recipient declined significantly.
- Medicaid, on the other hand, has been supplied more liberally— as have rent subsidies and food stamps.

Of course, such a redistribution of resources has the effect of keeping the poverty rate artificially high; the official rate therefore displays an increasingly distorted picture of reality. Furthermore, government expenditures for families with low incomes in real terms increased by almost 90 percent between 1978 and 1996.[17] The reduction in transfer payments has thus been more than compensated for by higher transfers in kind. Nevertheless, that is not reflected in the official poverty rate at all.

Taxes, finally, are also excluded from the calculation of the poverty rate. That's important because, in fact, low-income earners not only pay no income taxes, they even get money back from the Internal Revenue Service in the form of the Earned Income Tax Credit (EITC).

The EITC is a so-called negative income tax. Anyone who earns less than a certain amount receives a percentage of her income as a transfer. That subsidy can be as high as 40 percent.

The idea goes back to Nobel laureate Milton Friedman, and it is a charming idea, indeed. Friedman himself describes the benefits of this arrangement in the following way:

It is directed specifically at the problem of poverty. It gives help in the form most useful to the individual, namely, cash. It is general and could be substituted for the host of special measures now in effect. It makes explicit the cost borne by society. It operates outside the market. Like any other measures to alleviate poverty, it reduces the incentives of those helped to help themselves, but it does not eliminate that incentive entirely, as a system of supplementing incomes up to some fixed minimum would. An extra dollar earned always means more money available for expenditure.[18]

A key argument in favor of the negative income tax is that, as Friedman stresses, it does not stymie the incentive to work—a problem that usually comes along with traditional kinds of transfer payments. The German welfare system, for instance, is set up so that, at a certain income level, the marginal tax burden is 100 percent. In those cases, for every euro a German welfare recipient earns through work, he receives one euro less from the government. In other words, staying home is rewarded just as highly as earning additional money.[19]

With the negative income tax that is not the case. People who work more end up with more dollars in their pockets. For a family with two or more children, an additional earned dollar reduces the EITC by a maximum of 21 cents.[20]

About 20 million taxpayers make use of the EITC every year. Many of them are raised above the poverty line by this subsidy.[21] In 2002, for instance, the EITC reduced the number of poor Americans by almost 4.6 million.

While the EITC significantly ameliorates the problem of poverty in the United States, it does not remove it altogether. The question remains of why a sizable portion of the population cannot reach an income above the poverty level or, if it does, why it does so only with government assistance. And why for some does poverty indeed turn out to be a trap door after all?

Life Is Tougher for Ebony

Names matter. Life in America is more difficult if your name is "Ebony" or "Tyrone." Names like those or "Aisha" and "Kenya" are more popular among African Americans, whereas "Kristen" and "Brad" are more typical of the children of white Americans.

105

On the labor market, that difference is important. For example, an experiment conducted by economists Marianne Bertrand and Sendhil Mullainathan showed that, given identical résumés and written applications, a "Kristen" is 50 percent more likely than an "Aisha" to be invited to a job interview.[22]

African Americans are economically discriminated against in the United States, no question. What is questionable, however, is if it is discrimination alone that keeps African Americans behind. After all, discrimination over the last decades did not hinder a large number of African-American families from becoming part of the middle or even the upper class.

In 1960 the average full-time employed African American earned almost 40 percent less than his white counterpart. Nowadays the difference is 25 percent. In 1967 the income of 30 percent of married black couples was below the poverty line. In 2002 that number was 8.9 percent.[23]

Meanwhile, the share of African American households with a real gross income of more than $75,000 rose from 3.5 percent in 1970 to 12.9 percent in 2002. And 52 percent of all African-American households headed by a married couple reached over $50,000 in 2002.[24]

Thus, if discrimination indeed plays a crucial role, why does it stifle only some? Of course, it is possible that open discrimination has been replaced and compensated for by hidden discrimination (as is suggested by the experimental study mentioned above). But can that be the whole story?

Daniel Patrick Moynihan and the "Negro Family"

Daniel Patrick Moynihan, who passed away in March 2003, was the greatest intellectual in American politics and the greatest politician among America's intellectuals. He was a Harvard professor and ambassador to India and the United Nations before he represented New York state as a senator in Congress for 24 years.

The first time that the Democrat stepped into the limelight was in 1965. Back then he was a Labor Department official in Washington, D.C., and produced a report called "The Negro Family: The Case for National Action." Neglect or discrimination was not the predominant cause of the rampant poverty among urban blacks, argued the study now known as the "Moynihan report"; the cause was the decline of the African-American family. Moynihan wrote:

> Unless this damage is repaired, all the effort to end discrimination and poverty and injustice will come to little. . . . The family structure of lower class Negroes is highly unstable, and in many urban centers is approaching complete breakdown.[25]

Single mothers headed almost a quarter of African-American households, argued Moynihan. Among whites, the number of children born out of wedlock in 1963 was 3 percent; among African Americans it stood at almost 24 percent.

Since then, the problem has only been exacerbated. In 1950 two-thirds of all adult women were married, regardless of race. In 2002, 55 percent of all white women aged 15 years and older were married, but only 31 percent of African-American women were. Fourteen percent of all white families had a female head with no husband present; among black families, the share was 45 percent.[26]

The atomization especially of black families is a central reason for the continuation of poverty in America today:

- Forty years ago, only every fourth family that lived in poverty was a single-mother household. For more than 25 years now, that share has fluctuated around the 50 percent mark.[27]
- Families of married couples manage to move back above the poverty line after 3.9 months on average. It takes single-mother households 7.2 months to do so.[28]
- Single-mother households are more likely to be poor than other households, even if one or more family members work (Figure 9.2).[29]

Why the atomization of the family is largely an African-American problem will not be speculated upon here. What is interesting, however, is the extent to which America's cowboy capitalism had—or didn't have—a part in it.

Welfare Queens?

Americans have known federal welfare since 1933, but especially since Lyndon B. Johnson declared the War on Poverty in 1965, it has been much expanded. As mentioned before, real welfare expenditures between 1960 and 1973 more than quadrupled. The number

Figure 9.2
POVERTY RATES BY FAMILY TYPE AND PRESENCE OF WORKERS IN
THE UNITED STATES
(IN PERCENT, 2002)

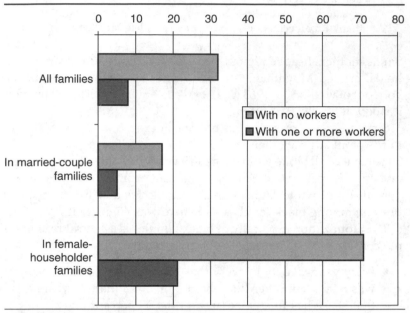

SOURCE: U.S. Census Bureau (2003a), p. 8.

of recipients increased in the same period from 3 to almost 11 million. By 1994 the number of welfare recipients had grown further, to 14.2 million.[30]

Welfare beneficiaries were long considered parasites. Ronald Reagan benefited in his 1980 presidential campaign not least from the "angry white men," traditionally more Democratic-leaning white manufacturing workers, who responded to rhetoric about "welfare queens."

The reality is different than was assumed. The "queens" are arguably victims of rather than parasites on the welfare state. Whether or not it was wise to expand the welfare system, the way in which it was expanded was highly questionable. For decades the system provided perverse incentives that, in combination, proved to be poverty traps for millions of American women and their children:

- Welfare allowed, in all its meagerness, for a modest life at home. But as a rule only those were eligible who had underage children and were *not* married. Especially women who, for lack of qualification, were able to make only a small income through work had a solid incentive to lead life as single, unemployed mothers. Only through the 1996 Welfare Reform Act was this incentive significantly diminished.
- Fathers, in turn, were basically invited to shirk their responsibilities. Although the government, since 1975, has increasingly tried to hold fathers financially responsible, the bureaucracies in 1998 didn't know the identity of the fathers of two of three kids in single-mother households. And even when paternity is established, child support is often not paid. Mothers meanwhile have little incentive to cooperate with officials, because child support is deducted from welfare payments.[31]

In the end it is almost impossible to prove or disprove what author George Gilder, among others, has asserted: that welfare created more poverty than it alleviated.[32] But that it for a long time set the wrong incentives is indicated by the change in the number of births to 15- to 19-year-old girls after welfare reform. From 1990 to 2002, it dropped by 28 percent. Among even younger girls and African Americans, the decline amounted to between 40 and almost 50 percent.[33]

* * *

America undoubtedly has a substantial poverty problem. At a closer look, however, it doesn't appear quite so dire. Fewer people are poor in America than statistics would have it, and those who are poor usually remain so for only a rather short time.

Many of the poor in America are immigrants from Latin America, people who would hardly be better off if they had been kept out. Finally, welfare, once hailed as an act of compassion, has contributed to the disintegration of the family in the United States, especially, for whatever reasons, among African Americans. That disintegration is one of the main reasons why there continues to be widespread poverty in America.

To attribute the problem of poverty squarely to U.S.-style cowboy capitalism is therefore at the very least rather daring. The problem is in large part the result not of the United States' largely unhampered capitalism but, quite the opposite, of a tragically failed attempt to restrain it.

10. "Just a Bunch of McJobs"

The service economy in the United States, dynamic as it may be, has mostly menial jobs to offer. Flipping burgers at McDonald's, stocking shelves at Wal-Mart, and asking "Paper or plastic?" at Safeway are often considered second-rate employment opportunities. Europeans refer to them disdainfully as "McJobs."

In addition to being disdainful, that attitude is also hypocritical. As economist and Nobel prize winner Joseph Stiglitz puts it: "You Europeans have a funny way of complaining. This is like saying: 'You Americans *did* create a lot of jobs. But they are lousy jobs. We Europeans didn't create any jobs, but if we had, they would have been good jobs.'"[1]

Furthermore, were the manufacturing jobs that were replaced by service jobs really much better, more challenging, exciting, or safer? Is the assembly line really preferable to the drive-through lane? And remember, 40 years ago hamburgers were grilled and diapers changed just as much. Only that was mother's job back then. But why is a job well regarded or at least acceptable when a housewife does it and stupid, banal, and even undignified when it is done for pay?

Nevertheless the question remains: Are the newly created jobs in America merely low-paying, low-skill jobs? Are job seekers relegated to working at McDonalds and thus to the bottom of the food chain?

The Erosion of the Minimum Wage

Ronald Reagan blasted the minimum wage as the cause of "more misery and unemployment than anything since the Great Depression." A minimum wage, the former president argued, is either too low to be meaningful or so high that the employment of people with low productivity declines.

There may be cases in which that reasoning doesn't hold up. If the minimum wage is very low to start with, an increase might induce low-qualified people to enter the labor market without leading to a decrease in employers' demand. However, as a rule, minimum wages tend to harm people with few skills by lowering the number of jobs available to them; that's one of the rather few things a vast majority of contemporary economists agree upon.

That's why most economists might have welcomed the fact that in the Reagan era the minimum wage was raised not even once. When Reagan left the White House in 1989, the purchasing power of the minimum wage had fallen by more than 25 percent. In the early and mid-1990s, the minimum wage was raised four times but not enough to reduce the gap between the minimum wage and the average wage to its traditional level. The minimum wage stood at around 45 percent of the average wage from the 1950s through the 1970s; now the minimum wage amounts to no more than 35 percent of the average wage. One of the results is that the number of Americans earning the minimum wage dwindled from 8.9 to 1.8 percent between 1980 and 2002.[2]

Even if it is hard to prove, it seems economically logical that the erosion of the minimum wage has contributed to the creation of millions of jobs for unskilled workers. For instance, the unemployment rate for women who had not finished high school was 8.9 percent in 2001. This compares to 11.5 percent in Germany, 14.0 percent in Italy, and 14.4 percent in France.[3]

Prime Jobs, Primarily

Still, it would be wrong to think of America's job machine as dependent on low-wage jobs. Burger flipping and grocery bagging are just a small part of the story. Even assuming that retail had not added a single job, employment in the United States would still have increased more during the 1980s and 1990s than it did, including retail, in France, Germany, or Italy.[4]

Numerous studies indeed have shown that the American economy has produced particularly high-quality jobs.[5] Steven Haugen and Randy Ilg did one such study. Those two Bureau of Labor Statistics economists created 90 data series using 10 major industries and 9 major occupations. They then divided those data series into three categories, each accounting for one-third of total employment in 1988: a group consisting of the occupation-industry categories with

Figure 10.1
EMPLOYMENT GROWTH BY EARNINGS GROUP IN THE UNITED
STATES
(PRECENTAGE CHANGE SINCE 1989)

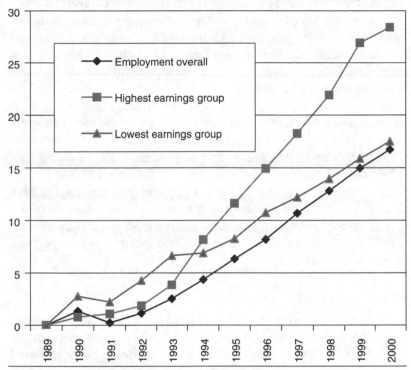

SOURCES: Ilg and Haugen (2000), pp. 24–25; and Ilg.

the highest median incomes, a middle-earnings group, and a lowest-earnings group.[6]

According to that categorization, employment in the lowest-earnings group grew by 17.5 percent between 1989 and 2000, only slightly faster than employment overall (Figure 10.1).[7] The group of high-income earners, however, grew disproportionately at 28.4 percent. Thus, the main characteristic of the job boom of the 1990s was not the creation of low-income jobs but the opposite. Of the net 17.3 million jobs newly created between 1989 and 2000, almost 60 percent, or 10.2 million, were in the top third of the income distribution.

That phenomenon is hardly new. It has obtained since at least the 1960s. And yet, the 1990s stand out: Far more than ever before employment growth was characterized by the creation of high-paying jobs. Take, for instance, America's information technology producers. That industry shed .6 million workers in 2001 and 2002, but in 2002 it still employed 1.2 million more people than it did in 1993. Reflecting the recession and the dot-com crash, average annual income for those workers did decline by more than $6,300 between 2000 and 2002. However, *average* annual pay still amounted to no less than $67,440 in 2002.[8]

And if one divides income groups into fifths instead of thirds, it can be shown that in the 1960s employment in the top fifth grew about 30 percent faster than in the second highest fifth. The numbers for the 1980s and 1990s are 40 and 80 percent, respectively.[9]

International comparison, too, fails to indicate that the United States created a disproportionately large number of low-paying jobs. That, at any rate, is suggested by the employment structure of the service sector. In 1998 the share of college graduates in that sector was 30.1 percent in the United States. In France it was 28.6 percent, in Italy a mere 16 percent.[10]

Working but Poor?

Often mentioned along with the "McJobs" are the "working poor." Indeed, official statistics classify millions of Americans as such. In 2001, 4.9 percent of employed Americans were declared "working poor." However, that statistic includes everyone who was in the labor force for at least 27 weeks in a given year. Therefore, not only the actually employed are counted but also people who are registered as job seekers. According to the official interpretation, in other words, you can be "working poor" even if you do not work at all.[11]

A single American who is employed full-time, year round, on the other hand, earns a gross income above the poverty line, even if he makes only the minimum wage. Households with two children and two full-time minimum wage earners, too, are above the poverty line.[12]

Indeed, in 2002 only 2.6 percent of full-time employees aged 16 and older had a household income beneath the poverty line. On

Figure 10.2
POVERTY RATES AND EMPLOYMENT IN THE UNITED STATES
(PERCENT IN POVERTY, PEOPLE AGED 16 AND OVER, 2002)

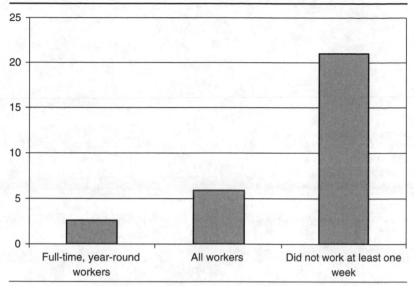

SOURCE: U.S. Census Bureau (2003a), p. 7.

the other hand, 21 percent of adults who did not work were poor (Figure 10.2).

In short, people who work regularly are, in all likelihood, not poor. Work is—in the United States as elsewhere—the best insurance against poverty. And as discussed in Chapter 9, the disposable income of low-wage earners is significantly above their gross income. The EITC, food stamps, public housing allowances, and employer benefits lift millions of Americans above the poverty line.

The phenomenon of the working poor *does* exist. But many thus labeled are either not working or not really poor. Finally, there is one more reason why it is doubtful that the working poor phenomenon is as big a social problem as the official numbers suggest: More than half of those who earned $5.15 an hour in 2001—53.4 percent to be specific—were 25 years old or younger.[13] It's not the single mom or the immigrant from Mexico who represents the typical minimum wage earner in America; it's the high school or college student from a middle-class family.[14]

11. "Moms Need to Work, Too"

Quite a lot of folks in America are rich. Many are poor. And in between there is . . . nobody. The perception that the United States is increasingly becoming a bipolar society with no middle class left is widespread on both sides of the Atlantic. Closely related to this idea is the notion that middle-class families can retain their standard of living only if Mom and Dad both work.[1]

That's not entirely off base. As pointed out in Chapter 10, the number of high-quality jobs has risen rapidly since 1989 while the number of low-income jobs has increased in sync with overall employment growth. This, in turn, implies that the growth of average-paying jobs has been weak. And indeed, the previously mentioned study by Haugen and Ilg confirms that. The number of jobs in the middle-earnings group grew by only 3.4 percent between 1989 and 2000.[2]

It's important to note, however, that although job creation in that segment lagged, the absolute number of those jobs did increase. Besides, what would have been a preferable alternative to that pattern of job creation? Persistently high unemployment among unskilled workers? Would it have been better if instead of high-paying service-sector jobs, the creation of traditional blue-collar worker jobs in manufacturing had been the predominant characteristic of the job market expansion?

If we look at the income of households, rather than individuals, there's no indication of a disappearing middle class anyway. Figure 11.1 divides American households into six income brackets. If the middle class were to disappear, the graph would resemble a wedge. The share of households that falls into either the low- or the high-income brackets would be on the rise at the expense of the middle. That obviously isn't what's been happening. In real terms, the share of households that have annual incomes of more than $75,000 increased continually over the last 30 years. Meanwhile the share of households that have less has been decreasing. There is simply no significant wedge to be detected.

Figure 11.1
PERCENT DISTRIBUTION OF HOUSEHOLDS' MONEY INCOME
(2002 DOLLARS)

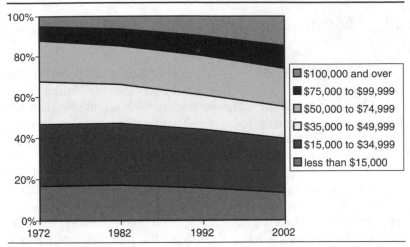

SOURCES: U.S. Census Bureau (2003), p. 17; and author's calculations.

But let's take a closer look. If "middle class," for instance, is defined as having a household income between $35,000 and $100,000 in 2002 dollars, then the middle class is, indeed, retreating. Under that definition, 46.2 percent of households belonged to the middle class in 1972. Ten years later the share was down to 44.9 percent. And though the share continued to decline over the following 20 years, it did so by only an additional .4 percentage point. Thus, although it is true that the percentage of households with medium incomes has been going down, it would be an exaggeration to speak of an eradication of the middle class.

Not accounted for in Figure 11.1, however, is the rise in two-income households over the last 30 years. Having two income earners in a family was a rarity in the 1970s. Today, it's common. Does that maybe mean that the only way millions of America's families are able to keep themselves from sliding out of the middle class is to have wives working, too?

Carly & Co.

The employment ratio of women in the United States grew rapidly in the 1970s and 1980s. It continued to rise in the 1990s, albeit

118

Figure 11.2
FEMALE LABOR FORCE PARTICIPATION IN ITALY, FRANCE,
GERMANY, AND THE UNITED STATES
(IN % OF FEMALE POPULATION 15–64 YEARS OLD)

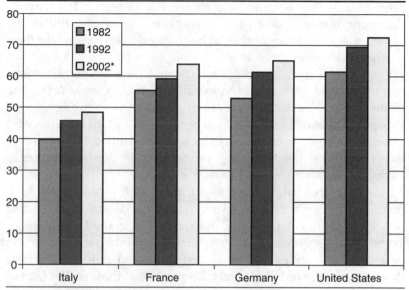

SOURCE: OECD (2003b), pp. 74–75, 170–71, 180–81, 230–31.
*The most recent numbers available for France and the United States are for 2001 and 2000, respectively.

less quickly. Indeed, the rise of the overall employment ratio, as discussed in Chapter 2, can be traced back almost entirely to the increasing number of working women.[3]

In France, Germany, and Italy, the labor force participation of women is significantly lower than in the United States (Figure 11.2). And the gap continues to widen. In America, the labor force participation rate of women increased by eleven percentage points between 1982 and 2002, whereas it grew by only some eight percentage points in France and Italy. Germany had slightly larger gains to record— the key reason, however, was the one-time effect of reunification with the formerly communist East Germany (which traditionally had a very high female employment ratio).

A higher ratio of women in the workforce is generally desirable. Or that's at least how the governments of the member states of the

European Union see it. The "European Employment Strategy," first concocted by the European Council in 1997, aims to increase the employment/population ratio of women to an EU-wide 60 percent in 2010.[4] And why not? When more women work, they don't usually do so because they have no other choice. For the entire 20th century, the proportion of women in the workforce grew steadily in the United States and most other industrialized countries while their husbands' incomes grew as well.[5]

Why then is the increasing employment ratio among American women viewed with suspicion in Europe and, on occasion, in the United States? Maybe it's because in recent decades it has been, to a disproportionate extent, married women with small children who entered the labor market in America. In the United States 6 of 10 wives with kids below the age of three are in the labor force; in Germany, the share is roughly half of that.[6]

However, that might have to do more with prohibitively high marginal tax rates for double-income families in Germany and better opportunities to balance work and family life in the United States. To be sure, as opposed to their German counterparts, American parents aren't entitled to government-sponsored childcare for their three- to six-year-olds. Still, only 2.3 percent of those in the United States who worked less than 35 hours a week in 2003 mentioned "childcare problems" as the reason for their short work week.[7]

Also, there can be no doubt that American women today are much closer to equal opportunity than German women. Take Allianz AG, Germany's largest insurance company, as an example. At Allianz Life USA, a subsidiary of Allianz based in Minneapolis, the share of women in management was 55 percent in October 2002. Of the 45 employees that the organization considers its top management, 42 percent, including the chief financial officer, were women. For comparison, at the Allianz group in Germany, the share of women in the top four management levels was 19 percent at the end of 2002.[8]

Women also are at the helm of a good number of major U.S. companies. Think of Carly Fiorina at Hewlett Packard, Anne Mucahy at Xerox, Pat Russo at Lucent, and Meg Whitman at Ebay. American women have even conquered what traditionally were male strongholds. Companies such as Bank One, Home Depot, J.P. Morgan, Merck, and Verizon have female CFOs. Every single one of the top 100 U.S. corporations (ranked by revenues) had at least one female director in 2003. And finally, women held 13.6 percent of all board seats in the "Fortune 500" companies in 2003; that represents an increase of more than 40 percent within just eight years.[9]

In Germany and Italy women in top corporate positions are still the exception. If you look at the 2003 "Fortune" list of the 50 "Most Powerful Women" outside the United States, you'll find France rather well represented with five entries. But only two Italian women made the list, compared with three from tiny Singapore. You will also find women from the Philippines, Saudia Arabia, and Turkey on that list but not a single German woman.[10]

Why Stay Home?

Statistics further strengthen the impression gotten from the anecdotal evidence:

- Since 1978 more American women than men have attended college. In 2000, 28 percent more women than men were enrolled; in graduate programs the difference was 37 percent.[11]
- In 2001 women were 46 percent of the employed in the United States. In the occupational category "managerial and professional specialty"—the one that typically goes along with the highest salaries—the share was a disproportionately high 50 percent.[12]
- The weekly income of women in 2002 was 78 percent that of men. Women working fewer hours on average cause a significant part of that discrepancy. If hourly wages in 2001 are considered, women earned an average of 85 percent of their male counterparts' wages. Compared with the past, this is a significant increase. In 1990 the ratio was still 78 percent; in 1980 it was 65 percent.[13]

No wonder surveys indicate that women increasingly leave home because they want to, not because they feel forced to. The share of American women who, given the choice, would rather work than be homemakers rose from 35 percent in 1974 to 48 percent in 1999. Over the same period, the share of those who would rather tend to the home and kids exclusively shrank from 60 to 44 percent.[14]

The idea that working women are a sign of desperation is further undermined by the findings of a study conducted by economists Chinhui Juhn and Kevin Murphy. They looked at trends in the 1970s and 1980s, the two decades in which the growth in female labor market participation was particularly strong. They found:[15]

- The big increase of women in the workforce can be traced back to an increasing number of wives of well-to-do men pushing into the labor market. These women typically earn high hourly wages.
- Meanwhile, among women whose husbands earned hourly wages in the bottom fifth of the distribution, the growth in labor market participation slowed down—contrary to the overall trend.
- In 1969 the annual incomes of working wives showed no correlation with the wages of their husbands. Wives of high-income earners earned above average wages, but they worked fewer hours than average. In the late 1980s, however, wives of high-income earners worked almost the same amount as wives of husbands with lower incomes.

Obviously, Juhn and Murphy conclude, economic necessity was not the predominant factor that caused women to enter the labor market in the 1970s and 1980s.[16]

Rather, their study gives further evidence of the fact that the American middle class is indeed *not* disappearing. Instead of being a sign of a middle class drifting into oblivion, working women represent the opportunities created by a plethora of new and well-paid jobs.

12. "Three Jobs Needed to Survive"

A hard day at work, eight hours on the assembly line and barely enough time to race home, change, get the kids to bed and a bite to eat. And off again, to his or her second job—perhaps as a cashier in the local supermarket or waiting tables. Such is the average day of hard-working Americans trying to make ends meet. At any rate, that's currently the favorite stereotype in Europe. Germany's top union leader, Michael Sommer, even professes to know that in the United States, "employees need three or four jobs to feed themselves."[1]

How many Americans actually *do* hold second or even third or fourth jobs? One in five? One in three? Maybe even 50 percent?

Not quite. In 2003, on average, 5.3 percent of all employed Americans had more than one job. That's not even 1 in 19. Most of those people worked either one full-time and one part-time job or two part-time jobs. Only .2 percent worked two full-time jobs.[2] And although the percentage of workers who held multiple jobs had been on the rise through the 1980s, it has receded noticeably since the mid-1990s and now is just slightly above the level that was common in the 1970s (Figure 12.1).

In other words, not only are Americans who work two or more jobs a small minority, there isn't a stable trend toward that phenomenon either.[3]

A Question of Incentives—And Opportunity

At the same time, it's clear that, according to the official statistics available, having two or more jobs is more common in the United States than it is in, say, Germany. In 2003 some 926,000 Germans had multiple jobs. That was a mere 2.4 percent of the employed.[4]

The actual percentage, however, is probably much closer to that in the United States. For one thing, the shadow economy is larger in Europe. Relative to official economic output, the illicit part of the economy is twice as large in Germany and France as it is in the United States. In Italy it's three times as large (see Chapter 6). Second,

123

Figure 12.1
MULTIPLE JOBHOLDING RATE IN THE UNITED STATES
(MULTIPLE JOBHOLDERS AS A PERCENT OF ALL EMPLOYED PERSONS;
MAY OF SELECTED YEARS, NOT SEASONALLY ADJUSTED)

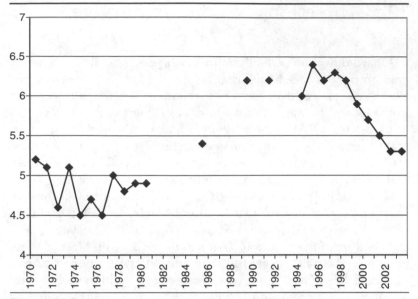

SOURCE: BLS.
NOTE: Data not available for missing years.

illegal immigration is without a doubt much more prevalent in the United States. That likely implies that in Europe a larger share of the shadow economy relies on natives seeking a tax-free second income rather than on illegals.

But even if we assume there to be fewer people working two jobs in Europe, is that an achievement of European-style capitalism?

Perhaps so. But perhaps the much higher marginal tax burdens are a major factor. The average wage earner in Germany has to pay almost two-thirds of any additional euro earned as taxes.[5] That might lead even those who would otherwise like to work a second job to refrain from seeking one. The magnitude of that effect is hinted at by the consequences of the German government's lifting of taxes on so-called mini-jobs in April 2003. The number of multiple jobholders rose markedly within months. For 2003 as a whole, it was 29 percent

Figure 12.2
REASONS FOR WORKING MORE THAN ONE JOB
(MAY 2001 CURRENT POPULATION SURVEY)

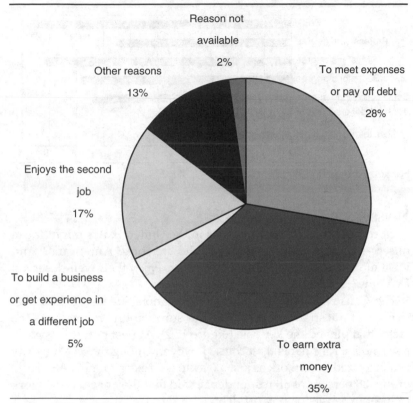

SOURCE: BLS (2002), p. 1.

above its 2002 level. And as of March 2004, the official German labor market researchers predicted another rise of 14 percent for the current year.[6]

Lack of opportunity is another issue. Perhaps more Germans would take a second job if only they could. In America it isn't a problem to work from nine to five and take an additional job after hours at, say, Wal-Mart or Home Depot. In Germany and other European countries, where stores must close in the early evening (or aren't allowed to open on Sundays), that's simply not possible.

125

Figure 12.3
MULTIPLE JOBHOLDERS BY EDUCATIONAL ATTAINMENT
(IN PERCENT, 1995 ANNUAL AVERAGES)

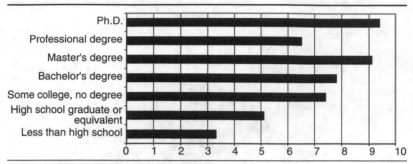

SOURCE: Amirault (1997), p. 10.

Struggling to Make Ends Meet?

Of course, holding multiple jobs in the United States might mean misery for millions of people. So who are those Americans? And what motivates them to labor while others enjoy their well-deserved free time?

The Census Bureau's "Current Population Survey" asked precisely that question in May 2001. Not surprisingly, money was the factor that played the key role (Figure 12.2). Almost two-thirds work a second job for financial reasons. However, among those, a majority characterized their work as just a way to earn extra money. A smaller group, 28 percent of all respondents, said that they needed the work to meet expenses or pay off debt.

Thus, only a small minority of Americans actually need to work multiple jobs to stay afloat. Those people are only 1.5 percent of all working Americans,[7] and the share is trending downward.[8] That leaves 98.5 percent of the workforce that either can or could do without second jobs and still be able "to feed themselves."

The educational attainment of those who work extra jobs supports that evaluation, as well.

Teachers, Not Hamburger Flippers

One might assume that the incidence of multiple jobholding is highest among unskilled laborers (with correspondingly low wages). In fact, the opposite is true. Generally speaking, the higher your

126

level of education, the more likely you are to take a second job. Among American college graduates, the rate of doing so is more than twice as high as it is among high-school dropouts (Figure 12.3). Professionals such as teachers, professors, psychologists, and accountants are the people who most commonly hold multiple jobs.[9]

That reinforces the point that multiple jobholding in a lot of cases is a matter of opportunity rather than necessity. Teachers, for example, often have rather flexible hours and periods in which they have much spare time.

And just where are those people struggling with three or more jobs that Germany's Sommer finds so symptomatic of American capitalism? Although they certainly do exist, they don't exactly represent a mass phenomenon. In 2003 a mere .34 percent of employed Americans were working three jobs, and only .06 percent held four or more.[10]

13. "Unemployed behind Bars"

If America's unemployed do not flock the streets, it's because they are behind bars. Or that's what politicians in Europe like to suggest. "Our unemployment would be 1.5 percentage points lower if we had as many people imprisoned here as there are in the United States," stated Werner Müller in early 2002.[1]

Of course, Müller, who at the time was Germany's minister of economic policy, was not suggesting that one ought to imprison unemployed Germans. Nor was he insinuating that Americans use their judicial system as an instrument of their labor market policies. He really could only have meant that the United States is not a suitable benchmark when it comes to low unemployment.

It's the War on Drugs, Stupid

Closely related to that is the European stereotype that Americans are more prone to criminal behavior than the citizens of other nations. It is true that many Americans are in prison. As mentioned in Chapter 6, in late 2002 the number was close to 2.2 million—four times as many as in 1980. That constitutes 700 people incarcerated per 100,000—a higher rate than anywhere else in the world.[2]

It's also true that in the 1980s the rate of thefts, robberies, burglaries, and assaults was higher in the United States than anywhere else in the industrialized world.[3] And intentional homicides are still more prevalent than in other industrialized countries: in 1999 the homicide rate was 4.55 per 100,000 people in contrast to rates between 1.22 and 1.63 in Germany, France, and Italy.[4]

However, crime rates in the United States have been trending downward for years now. The International Crime Victimisation Survey (ICVS), the most encompassing international study, has shown that in 1999 the United States actually compared favorably in a number of categories with the 16 other countries surveyed. It ranked 6th in burglaries and attempted burglaries, 13th in robberies, and 17th in assaults. Car theft is twice as common in France; in

England and Wales, it is three times more common than in the United States.[5]

Thus, if there are so many more people behind bars in America than elsewhere, nowadays it's not mainly caused by high crime rates. Rather, the key reason seems to be that punishment in the United States is extraordinarily severe. Indeed, there is no European counterpart for the strict prosecution of drug consumption or "Three Strikes" laws.

Müller's Fuzzy Math

Perhaps the United States benefits from those draconian punishments through a reduced crime rate. The effect on unemployment, however, is marginal at best.

Prison inmates are indeed not included in unemployment statistics. But as a tool to control unemployment prisons would be very expensive. For corrections alone (that is, excluding the cost for police and the judicial system), the government spends about $29,000 annually per prisoner.[6]

Most important, any positive effect that that "investment" may have on unemployment numbers would be of a temporary nature only. In the longer run, locking away delinquents for long periods of time is instead likely to *increase* unemployment.

That's because it's difficult, or at least more difficult than before, for anyone released from prison to find a decent job. He or she encounters prejudices and has all the same problems that the long-time unemployed face (see Chapter 17). That's likely to be true especially in times of rapid technological progress (see Chapters 15 and 16). Furthermore, reintegration has become more difficult since the mid-1990s when Congress ended welfare state entitlements for anyone convicted of drug abuse.[7] More than twice as many Americans as are actually imprisoned face these kinds of problems. At the end of 2002, 4.7 million people in the United States were on probation or parole.[8]

What's more, that a rising prison population could even temporarily spell significant relief for the U.S. labor market is doubtful. Müller implied that all prisoners, were they free, would be unemployed. That argument is akin to the claim that in any economy only a certain amount of labor is available. Reality, however, paints a different picture (see Chapter 2).

Indeed, at the time of their arrest, about a third of America's prisoners held jobs.[9] Using that statistic, labor market economists Lawrence Katz and Alan Krueger have calculated the effect of the prison boom on the U.S. labor market.

Their conclusion is that the growing number of inmates made only a minor contribution to the reduction in unemployment between 1985 and 1998. In 1998 unemployment was .1 to .2 percentage points lower than it would have been if the prison population had remained the same.

That in turn indicates that the effect on unemployment Müller mentioned might actually exist. But if it does, it very likely does so only in the short term. And even then, it's a tiny fraction of what he suggested.

14. "The Doctor Won't See Them Now ..."

Europeans are very familiar with the U.S. health care system. After all, there are movie theaters on both sides of the Atlantic. The French and Germans saw Helen Hunt as a mother who can't afford the necessary treatment for her son in *As Good As It Gets*. They also watched *John Q*, in which Denzel Washington plays a father who tries to extort the heart transplant his son needs by taking hostages.

Indeed, the lack of universal access to decent health care can with some justification be considered the United States' biggest social problem. At least it is a problem that affects many people, including lots of middle-class families.

Infant mortality is a telling example: In 2001 the rate was seven deaths per thousand live births. In France, Germany, and Italy as well as considerably poorer countries such as the Czech Republic or Slovenia, just four of every thousand infants died.[1] And having almost a seventh of the population living without health insurance policies, as is the case in the United States, is unheard of in Western Europe.

A central reason for that plight is the cost. The United States has the most costly health care system in the world (Figure 14.1). It devoured 13.9 percent of the entire economic output in 2001. For comparison, the German health care system, which by international standards is also expensive, cost 10.8 percent of GDP.

That raises the question of why the U.S. health care system is so expensive and so much more expensive than any other.

This chapter will not try to give a comprehensive answer. Rather, it will address two features that distinguish the U.S. system markedly from its counterparts in all other industrialized countries: the cost of pharmaceuticals and the tort system.

High Drug Prices Are Good for You

Prices that the pharmaceutical industry may charge for its patent products are kept artificially low everywhere else in the world

Figure 14.1
INTERNATIONAL COMPARISON OF HEALTH EXPENDITURES
(PERCENT OF GDP, 2001)

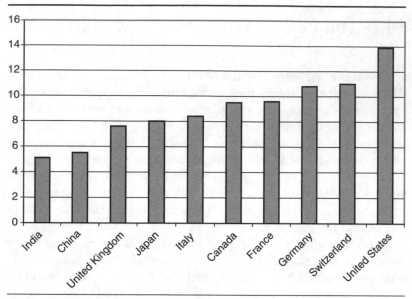

SOURCE: WHO (2003), pp. 170–76.

through either direct price controls, profit limits, or—as in Germany—upper limits on reimbursement.

The one big exception is the United States. Here, prices for patent drugs are mostly left to the forces of supply and demand. The result is significantly higher prices. Depending on the current exchange rate, Pfizer, for example, gets twice or three times the wholesale price for its cholesterol-lowering drug Lipitor in the United States that it gets in France, Germany, or Italy. Even though in the United States the amount of drugs prescribed per capita was 27 percent below the OECD average in 1996, expenses for drugs were 41 percent above the average.[2]

Of the total expenditures for health care in the United States, drugs account for just one eighth. But for more than 20 years drugs have been the primary reason for the climbing cost of health care. In the 1990s expenses for prescription drugs grew at twice the rate of total expenditures for health care. More than 40 percent of that growth was attributable to "blockbuster" drugs that were approved after 1992.[3]

Thus, according to IMS Health, a consultancy, in 2003 the global pharmaceutical industry made 49 percent of its revenue in the United States; despite its larger population, the EU accounted for only 25 percent.[4] The share of profits earned on the U.S. market is, given the higher profit margins, undoubtedly even much larger.

Jean-François Dehecq, head of the French pharmaceutical company Sanofi-Synthelabo, describes the situation as follows:

> Step-by-step, the profitability of European markets is decreasing, and we're depending on the U.S. more and more. At the beginning of a drug's life cycle, it isn't so bad. But each year we increase prices a little in the U.S. And each year we have to decrease a little in Europe. . . . After a few years down the line, it's a disaster.[5]

Is this a reflection of the influence of the pharmaceutical lobby in the United States? Presumably. That the industry is not required to make so-called solidarity contributions, as it is forced to on a by now regular basis in Germany, may well have something to do with the amount of political donations that the Pfizers and Mercks dole out.

But that doesn't necessarily mean that the drug prices charged in the United States aren't justified. In order to be able to assess that, one should have a rough idea of how drugs affect the quality of life.

To make such estimates and attach a monetary value to them is a tricky undertaking. After all, for such an assessment one has to estimate how much money a human life is worth. A primitive and wholly unsatisfactory method is to take as a yardstick the income a person will presumably earn over her lifetime.

A more elegant and appropriate alternative for measuring the worth of a life is to figure out how much money people would be willing to pay to stay alive for an additional year. That can't be measured directly. But it is possible to assess the willingness of people to take risks. That willingness in turn can be measured by the extra wages employees demand in return for bearing an increased likelihood of dying on the job.

Economists Kevin Murphy and Robert Topel have used that method for the United States. Their conclusion is that the life of an

American is worth about $5 million and every additional year between $150,000 and $200,000. (Those estimates are a bit higher than others but do not differ greatly.)[6]

On that basis Murphy and Topel calculated how the improvements in life expectancy affected the prosperity of Americans between 1970 and 1990. To call the results huge would be to put it mildly. In 1992 dollars, the increased life expectancy was the equivalent of an *annual* increase in wealth of $2.8 trillion. In the future, further vast gains are to be expected. Reducing the death rate from heart disease or cancer by just 1 percent, for instance, would further increase American wealth by the equivalent of $50 billion. Note that all those calculations do not even include the fact that many new drugs or treatments may not extend life but improve its quality, for instance by causing fewer side effects or easing pain.

Murphy and Topel conclude that "the gains are so large that it is hard to believe that the return to health intervention was not enormous." In comparison, the expenditures for research and development of new drugs seem "minute."[7]

Admittedly, not all of that increase in wealth can be attributed to new drugs or other medical treatments alone. Better education and healthier diets, for instance, may have played an important role, too. But modern econometrics makes it possible to distinguish between the influence new drugs have had and the influence of factors such as education, income, nutrition, and lifestyle. That's exactly what Frank Lichtenberg has done.

The health economist from Columbia University isolated the effect that new drugs had in 52 countries. He considered only drugs that were new in the sense that they contain new chemical entities. Those drugs, Lichtenberg found, were responsible for no less than 40 percent of the increase in life expectancy between 1986 and 2000.

If that is put into relation with the $250 that industrialized countries spend annually per capita on pharmaceutical R&D, then a cautious calculation reveals that it costs $4,500 per capita in R&D to improve the general life expectancy by a full year. That is clearly a tiny sum compared with the value of an additional year of life.[8]

Those results imply:

- Today's investments in pharmaceutical progress yield a very high social return. As Lichtenberg puts it, "Outlays for new drugs are plainly an incredible bargain."[9]

- Investments in the development of new drugs are smaller, probably much smaller, than the well-understood self-interest of mankind should demand. "The potential gain from additional improvements in health care," Murphy and Topel write, "is gigantic."[10]
- Because ultimately only the prospect of higher profits can get the pharmaceutical industry to invest more in R&D, it's not the Americans who pay too much for their drugs. It's the French, the Germans, and the Italians who pay too little.
- As long as today's level of investment is worthwhile only because of the high profit margins in the United States, other countries free ride. Only high prices in the United States guarantee that artificially low prices in Germany and elsewhere don't choke off this highly valuable research.

Doctors on the Defensive

Samuel Desiderio is an unfortunate young man deserving of everyone's empathy. After he underwent surgery in the New York Presbyterian Hospital in 1990, doctors failed to notice that pressure was building up in his brain. Not even four years old at the time, he suffered permanent brain damage. A jury awarded Desiderio $140 million in damages—a ruling that has since been upheld by the New York's State Court of Appeals.[11]

Desiderio's lawsuit may have been as justified as the amount of damages that he received. And who could be against the right of victims to pursue malpractice through the courts?

However, malpractice lawsuits have become a national pastime in the United States. And clearly, when damages reach, as in Desiderio's case, $100 million plus, they become a major cost factor. Indeed, as the amount of compensation has grown, U.S. liability laws have become one of the main culprits for the explosion of health care costs.[12]

In 2001, 39 percent of suing patients whose cases were decided by a jury were successful. More than half of those were rewarded $1 million or more—twice as many as in 1996.[13]

What's more, the risk exposure for the defendants is entirely impossible to calculate. How high damages will be in any given case can't be predicted because in most states there are no caps. Whether the sum ends up having six or eight digits depends more

137

on the whim of the moment than on anything else. In Europe, by contrast, no such "lawsuit lottery" exists; damages are much lower and, at least as important, much more predictable.

The lawsuit craze in the United States has already undermined the trust between doctors and patients. After all, every wrong statement could bring about a multi-million-dollar lawsuit. New therapies and drugs are used only hesitatingly, because from the doctor's point of view, everything new and unknown carries some risk of a lawsuit.[14]

Also, the cost of malpractice insurance is rising dramatically. In Florida premiums for an Ob/Gyn run $210,000 a year. In California, where tort liability is more restricted, the very same insurance costs $57,000.[15]

In some places, such excessive premiums have already threatened the availability of medical care. Gynecologists refuse to assist in childbirth, and entire obstetric units have been closed. Specialists such as neurosurgeons, emergency doctors, and urologists quit their jobs or move their practices out of states that are known to hand out extraordinarily high damages to patients. By early 2004 the American Medical Association had declared 19 states emergency regions; tort law reform tops the AMA's wish list.[16]

Critics such as New York lawyer Philip Howard, founder of the reform movement Common Ground, estimate the cost of excessively high insurance premiums and lawsuits at $10 billion annually.[17] And that's not all. Add to that the costs of "defensive medicine"— treatments that are exclusively or chiefly aimed at protecting doctors from lawsuits rather than helping patients. Defensive medicine is not only a waste of resources, it can also harm the patient—for example, when a doctor shies away from promising but risky treatments.[18]

Just how widespread the practice of defensive medicine is in the United States was shown by a survey of 300 doctors in March 2002. Forty-one percent of the respondents admitted to prescribing more drugs than medically necessary in order to avoid lawsuits. Seventy-four percent said that they sent patients to specialists more often than necessary, and 79 percent declared that, by their own reckoning, they ordered too many tests.[19]

Estimating the cost of that problem is difficult, because in any single case it can't be determined from afar what motivations caused a doctor to prescribe a certain treatment. However, economists Daniel Kessler and Mark McClellan have found a solution. In a study that won the Kenneth Arrow Award in Health Economics, they looked at how the treatment of heart patients in states with very lawsuit-conducive climates differed from treatment in states where liability is more limited. The underlying presumption is that to the extent that increasingly expensive tort liability is correlated with the intensity of medical care, but without positive health outcomes, physicians are practicing defensive medicine.[20]

Their findings were that even modest reforms would eliminate large parts of the problem. Reforms that directly limit liability, such as caps on damage awards or the abolition of punitive damages, could reduce hospital expenditures by 5 to 9 percent without any negative effect on the well-being of patients. The tort system burdens the U.S. health care system with a price tag of "well over $50 billion per year," Kessler and McClellan concluded. More recent estimates of the cost come to twice as much.[21]

* * *

The two features described—the lack of price controls and the out-of control tort system—are in good measure responsible for the high cost of the U.S. health care system. If, for instance, liability laws were reformed and at the same time expenditures for drugs were cut in half through price controls, America's health care expenditures as a share of GDP could be reduced by about two percentage points. That would leave the U.S. health care system hardly more expensive than the German one, making health insurance more affordable for millions of Americans (at the price, as argued above, of a very high cost in terms of pharmaceutical progress forgone.)[22]

An American-style tort system may be an integral element of a relatively unrestricted capitalist system. The fewer regulations people face up-front, the larger will arguably be the need to rein in negative developments after the fact, that is, through the court system. That the United States is a more litigious country than others may be, in this regard, only natural.

But the American tort system—as it has developed, and not only in regard to medical matters—has created such excesses and uncertainties that it can't be considered merely the unavoidable price to be paid for relatively unregulated markets. To the extent that tort liability is responsible for insufficient health care coverage, it's a case of collective self-mutilation, not the price that a country pays for a dynamic economic system.

However, the absence of price controls on patent drugs *is* clearly typical of "cowboy capitalism." And, to the extent that high drug prices lead to millions of uninsured people, that is a downside of the American economic model. To simplify: By deciding against price controls, Americans made a decision in favor of highly valuable pharmaceutical progress, implicitly accepting, however, that that decision might drive up overall health care expenditures, thereby raising health insurance payments to a level that some people could not afford.

Such a decision may not be reconcilable with the European mind-set about the role of the welfare state. But if the benefits of drug developments are even close to being as large as the above-mentioned studies suggest, no one in free-riding Europe should hope that Americans ever reverse their decision.

PART III

UNEQUAL AND UNJUST

15. Income Inequality—Tectonic Shifts or What?

The rich get richer and the poor get poorer. That view is widespread on both sides of the Atlantic. In the United States 72 percent of the population hold that opinion; in Germany, 86 percent do.[1]

At least from a global perspective, that statement is simply not correct. Income inequality is not on the rise. Indeed, the opposite is true: it's going down. The rise of China and India especially contributed to a decline of the gap in the 1980s and 1990s. According to one study, incomes worldwide are distributed more evenly than they have been since 1910.[2]

The development *within* industrialized countries, however, looks different. Since the mid-1980s, inequality has been on the rise in most industrialized countries, and a clear trend to the contrary is nowhere to be seen.[3]

Tectonic Shifts

What makes America special is not that income had always been distributed more unequally than in other Western countries. In France, for example, the top 10 percent of taxpayers had a significantly higher share of total income in the 1950s and 1960s.[4]

What does make America special is what Princeton economist Paul Krugman calls "tectonic shifts": an unusually strong *rise* in the inequality of income distribution. That trend started in the middle of the 1970s and slowed down only in the second half of the 1990s.[5]

A common way of displaying an income distribution is shown in Figure 15.1. American households are separated into five equal parts. The lowest fifth represents the 20 percent with the lowest income; the highest fifth represents the 20 percent with the highest income. The basis for that division is "money income," a measure that includes income before taxes but does not reflect, among other things, employer-paid benefits and capital gains (see Chapter 7).

Figure 15.1
SHARES OF AGGREGATE INCOME RECEIVED BY EACH FIFTH OF HOUSEHOLDS IN THE UNITED STATES
(IN PERCENT; HOUSEHOLDS AS OF MARCH OF THE FOLLOWING YEAR)

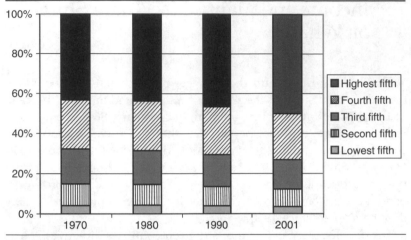

SOURCE: U.S. Census Bureau (www.census.gov).

The figure shows how the income shares of the fifths changed between 1970 and 2001. The shares of the four lower quintiles have receded to the advantage of the top 20 percent. Given a change of statistical measurement in the early 1990s, the actual shift has not been as pronounced as shown here. Especially the lowest-income households have probably experienced a more positive change.[6]

That doesn't alter the big picture though. The share of income earned by high-income households grew significantly—at the expense of all others. With regard to income distribution, a gap has opened since the 1970s.

Figure 15.1, however, merely indicates that the rich have gotten richer. It doesn't show that the other income groups have lost ground. To get a more complete picture of the shift in income inequality over the last decades, it's therefore advisable to take a closer look at what happened. Figure 15.2 shows income ratios. First, take a household that makes a gross income equal to the average of the tenth percentile of the population. In other words, the household earns less than 90 percent of the households with the highest income but more than the 9 percent with the lowest. That household income

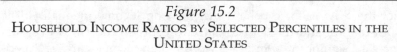

Figure 15.2
HOUSEHOLD INCOME RATIOS BY SELECTED PERCENTILES IN THE
UNITED STATES

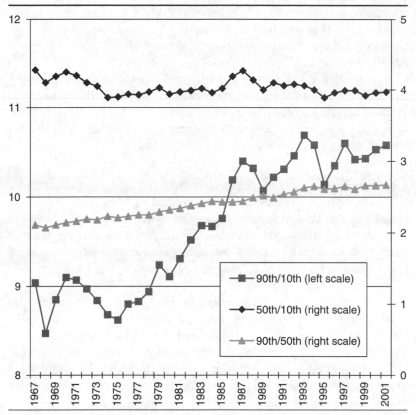

SOURCE: U.S. Census Bureau (www.census.gov).

is put in relation to the median income (50th percentile) and the household income in the 90th percentile. As a result, we get two standard measures of inequality—the 90th-to-10th percentile ratio and the 50th-to-10th percentile ratio; in addition, Figure 15.2 also displays the 90th-to-50th percentile ratio.[7]

What is clear is that the 50th-to-10th percentile ratio does *not* show a clear trend. If anything, the ratio has been trending down slightly since the end of the 1980s. It stands to reason that low-income households losing ground vis-à-vis average-income households was

145

not the driving force behind the growing income inequality. The 90th-to-10th and the 90th-to-50th percentile ratios, however, *did* increase significantly. In other words, high-income earners experienced disproportionately big gains over the last 30 or so years. Again, the conclusion is that income inequality has increased not because the poor have gotten poorer (see Chapter 7) but because the rich have gotten richer.

The trend toward increasing income inequality has weakened considerably, though. In 2001 the 90th-to-50th percentile ratio stood at 2.67, barely higher than in 1994 when it was 2.65. The 90th-to-10th ratio was even lower in 2001 than in 1993 when it reached a record level (10.58 vs. 10.69).

Tectonic Shifts?

When incomes diverge it is only natural to assume that so does consumption. That, however, is not the case.

Distribution of income and consumption are shown in Figure 15.3 using the Gini index. The Gini index is a statistical measure of concentration that takes on a higher value the higher the inequality of distribution of a variable is.[8]

As a look at Figure 15.3 shows, income disparity grew in the 1970s. That was followed by a lateral trend as early as the mid-1980s, not just since the mid-1990s as Figure 15.2 indicates.[9]

More important, however, is a different conclusion: The increasingly unequal income distribution was not paralleled by an increase in consumption inequality. The Gini index for consumption was, as of 1998, only marginally above that of 30 years ago.

Evidently the relation between income and consumption has loosened. To put it differently: A low income can no longer be equated with a low standard of living.[10] The statistics cited in Chapter 9 that show that the fifth of earners with the lowest income spent $2.29 for every dollar of net earnings in 2002 support that conclusion.

How the disconnect between income and consumption came about is difficult to say. One possibility is that the stagnation of low incomes is merely a statistical phenomenon. It could be that the incomes of the poor are being underestimated by statistics more than they used to be—perhaps because of a growing shadow economy or because incomes, to a larger extent than before, are not declared so as to not lose eligibility for transfers.[11]

146

Figure 15.3
INCOME AND CONSUMPTION INEQUALITY IN THE UNITED STATES
(GINI INDEXES)

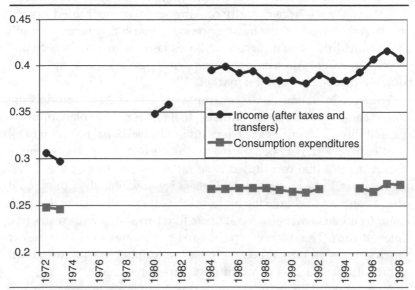

SOURCE: Krueger and Perri (2003).
NOTE: Data not available for missing years.

Moreover, there is reason to believe that Americans can handle reductions in income more easily than in the past. If, for instance, a job loss is considered temporary, it might barely restrict consumption. Economist Milton Friedman alluded to that possibility when he introduced his permanent income hypothesis in the 1950s. According to that hypothesis, people do not make their habits of consumption dependent on short-term income fluctuations but adjust them to expected long-term incomes.[12]

That might be easier to accomplish nowadays than it used to be. Even low-income earners, for example, have significant savings. The average *net* worth of a household in the lowest quintile of income earners was $52,600 in 2001. More than half of that, $28,500, was invested in nonretirement stock and mutual fund holdings and could thus be easily converted into cash.[13]

In addition, credit cards and the habit of paying in installments have made it easier for people with low incomes to obtain credit.

147

Of course, one could assume that credit card companies hand out their products with little scrutiny of the creditors' solvency, driving low-income earners into ruin by the millions. Chapter 8, however, has shown that a large majority of Americans are not buried in debt at all. And even with the most aggressive marketing tactics, it can't be assumed that credit card companies issue their products to just about everyone. Any company that would do such a thing would quickly disappear from the market.

To see why credit cards became available even to low-income Americans, it seems more realistic to look for an explanation the plausibility of which does not depend on the irrational behavior of all parties involved. For openers, there was the decision of the Supreme Court in 1978 that constituted a de facto dismantling of the states' usury laws. In *Marquette v. First Omaha Service Corp.*, the Court ruled that a bank could charge the highest interest rate allowed in its home state to all customers—even if they lived in states with restrictive interest caps. This allowed credit card companies to charge higher interest rates. In turn, it became possible for people with low credit ratings to have access to admittedly expensive credit.[14]

Technological innovations, too, enter the picture. Information and communication technologies allow for much easier checks on credit history and credit worthiness. When banks and credit card companies can check a potential customer's credit history over long periods, it puts people who have low incomes but have long been reliable debtors in a better position.

Third, economists Dirk Krueger and Fabrizio Perri have found empirical evidence for a causal relation between the growing disparity in incomes and the availability of credit cards.[15] The idea behind this is that whenever structural change is sped up while at the same time the social safety net is either shrunk or not expanded, the risk in taking short-term losses in disposable income increases. Under those circumstances, it becomes more important to have access to credit.

That in turn means that the incentive to not service debt decreases for debtors. To put it differently: The most important sanction available to creditors—denial of future credit to those who have defaulted on their payments—is strengthened. Lenders who are aware of that connection are more likely to grant credit more liberally than before.

To sum up, it can be said that income inequality has increased substantially since the 1970s. This was mostly triggered by the disproportionate gains of high-income earners. At the same time, it did not lead to a significant increase in inequality of consumption. That might also be the case because income redistribution is much more focused on helping the needy in the United States than in continental Europe.

European Welfare States Out of Control

So far, this chapter has looked at income before taxes. What really counts for households, however, is how much of their gross income is left after the government is through redistributing.

OECD economists Michael Förster and Mark Pearson did one study that shows how gross incomes and disposable incomes differ in 18 industrialized countries. The authors calculated "equivalent disposable household incomes" per individual of the working-age population. That number includes gross earnings, gross capital and self-employment incomes as well as all kinds of cash transfers; income and payroll taxes are subtracted. Förster and Pearson attain "equivalence" by taking into consideration the economies of scale that bigger households realize—in the sense that a four-person household attains a higher standard of living than two two-person households that, taken together, have the same income.[16]

Förster and Pearson created three income groups for the 18 countries: the 30 percent of the population with the lowest equivalent disposable income, the 30 percent with the highest, and the remaining 40 percent in the middle.

Such a grouping brings to light the fact that the distribution of market incomes is surprisingly similar in the 18 countries. In the mid-1990s the lowest third received only between 6 and 12 percent of total income. The upper 30 percent got between 50 and 60 percent in most countries. That was true for the United States, Italy, France, and Germany, with Italy and the United States leaning toward the unequal ends of the ranges and France and Germany toward a more balanced distribution (Figure 15.4A).

Progressive America

The tax codes level some of the differences. Mostly high-income taxpayers finance the budget in the United States. In fiscal year 2001

149

Figure 15.4A
DISTRIBUTION OF MARKET INCOME IN THE UNITED STATES, ITALY, FRANCE, AND GERMANY
(SHARES OF TOTAL MARKET INCOME* BY DIFFERENT INCOME GROUPS OF THE WORKING-AGE POPULATION, MID-1990s***)

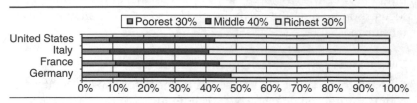

Figure 15.4B
DISTRIBUTION OF TAX PAYMENTS IN THE UNITED STATES, ITALY, FRANCE, AND GERMANY
(SHARES OF DIRECT INCOME TAXES** PAID BY DIFFERENT INCOME GROUPS OF THE WORKING-AGE POPULATION, MID-1990s***)

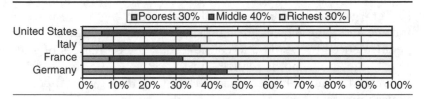

Figure 15.4C
DISTRIBUTION OF CASH TRANSFERS IN THE UNITED STATES, ITALY, FRANCE, AND GERMANY
(SHARES OF CASH TRANSFER BENEFITS RECEIVED BY DIFFERENT INCOME GROUPS OF THE WORKING-AGE POPULATION, MID-1990s***)

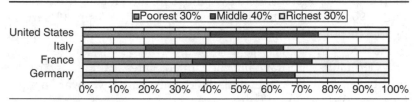

SOURCE: Förster and Pearson (2002), pp. 21, 31.
*Includes gross earnings, capital income, and self-employment income.
**Includes employees' payroll taxes.
***United States, 1995; Italy, 1993; France, 1994; Germany, 1994.

almost 65 percent of federal income tax came from the 10 percent of private households with the highest gross income. In Germany, by contrast, the top 10 percent contributed less than half of the intake. Furthermore, the 50 percent of households with lower-than-average incomes contributed almost 9 percent of German income tax revenues whereas they contributed only 4 percent in the United States.[17]

That comparison is to be taken with some caution. Payroll taxes are not considered here, nor is the fact that Germans do not have any direct personal income taxes at the state and local levels. The survey by Förster and Pearson does, however, confirm that America's low-income households pay relatively little in taxes in comparison with their share of disposable income. The amount that is shouldered by the "rich" is a bit lower than in France but higher than in Italy and far higher than in Germany (Figure 15.4B).

Thus, the American tax code burdens high-income households even more heavily than the Italian and especially the German ones. In that sense, it turns out to be more progressive.

And in reality, the differences in the transatlantic comparison are likely to be even bigger than is hinted at in Figure 15.4B. That's so because indirect taxes such as sales and gasoline taxes are clearly higher in continental Europe. Those taxes affect everyone equally, independent of income, and therefore hit the poor harder than the rich.

That the U.S. tax code *appears* more progressive doesn't mean it actually *is* more progressive. Of course it isn't. Marginal tax rates are lower in the United States than in France, Germany, and Italy, and the top tax brackets are reserved for much higher incomes.

In the end, the reason for the discrepancy in the transatlantic comparison remains an object of speculation. Two explanations, though, come to mind: The progressive nature of the tax codes is undermined by tax exemptions that favor high-income earners, especially in Germany. It is also likely that the discrepancy reflects the incentives to work fostered by low marginal tax rates in the United States and the disincentives to work fostered by much higher ones in Europe.

Redistribution from the Better-Off—To the Better-Off

Of course, the comparison is only complete when, in addition to gross income and taxes, we look at what the state gives back to

151

citizens. Ignoring transfers in kind, a look at cash transfers shows that on average the 18 countries dole out just 36.2 percent of benefits to the poorest 30 percent while no less than 25.9 percent goes to the richest 30 percent.

That the well-to-do receive such a large share might be in part a consequence of the fact that many transfers, such as cash benefits for households with children, are often distributed to all eligible recipients without regard to their income level. However, it seems to be the case that some transfers, deliberately or not, in fact favor primarily the rich.

Whatever the reason may be, it's the result that matters. Förster and Pearson surmise that redistribution via cash transfers does "not have a very different effect on final income inequality from paying everyone in the population a fixed amount of benefit, regardless of income level."[18]

The rich would even lose out under such a scenario in Germany and Italy where the upper 30 percent receive a disproportionate 30.7 and 34.5 percent of the cash transfers, respectively (Figure 15.4C). The lower 30 percent in contrast get very little more in Germany (31.7 percent). In Italy, they get a lot less (20.5 percent).

One would assume that the primary responsibility of the welfare state is to insure its citizen against the greater risks in life. If that is indeed the goal, then Germany's and Italy's redistribution machines are clearly highly inefficient.

Not even the more modest, more easily achievable goal of simply redistributing from the top to the bottom is reached in Germany or Italy. While there is certainly plenty of redistribution going on, there is obviously rather little redistribution from rich to poor. What remains, however, is paralysis caused by high tax burdens.

Hey, Big Spender

In Anglo-Saxon countries, including the United States, the situation looks quite different. Transfers are aimed more specifically at the truly needy. In the United States 41.4 percent of the cash transfers go to the poorest 30 percent of the population. That may not seem to some to be a whole lot, but it's more than in France and a lot more than in Germany or Italy.

It therefore seems that countries with small governments tend to spend their revenue more efficiently. That is exactly what a study by Ludger Schuknecht and Vito Tanzi points out. The German-Italian economist duo partitioned 17 countries into three groups: one group of countries in which government expenditures amounted to more than half of GDP in 1990 (for example, Italy and Sweden); one group in which the spending level was between 40 and 50 percent of GDP (for example, Germany and France); and finally those where governments restrained themselves to spending less than 40 percent of GDP (for example Great Britain, Japan, and the United States).[19]

Comparison of those three groups shows:

- The differences between spending levels are explained almost entirely by higher transfers, subsidies, and debt-servicing costs in the countries with large governments. The levels of public investment, on the other hand, don't differ much.
- Using the Human Development Index of the United Nations as the yardstick (see Chapter 7), the countries with the lowest spending levels have the highest standards of living.
- The distribution of disposable incomes is more even in the countries with big government. In the countries with lean government, however, redistribution of market income through taxation and benefits increases the share of total income that goes to the poorest 40 percent of households by 2.1 percentage points. In big-government countries the increase is a mere 0.6 point bigger—even though the tax collectors claim roughly 20 percentage points more of GDP.

To attain its social and economic objectives, a modern economy does not need XXL-sized government, conclude Schuknecht and Tanzi. The same goals, they believe, could be achieved "with intelligent policies"—and a "level of spending ranging from, say, 25 percent to 35 percent of GDP."[20]

16. And the Culprit Is . . . Progress

You might consider an increase in income inequality a bad thing, a violation of economic justice. But wait a minute. First, isn't equal *opportunity* a more fundamental aspect of justice? Isn't inequality of incomes and wealth that stems from unequal access to educational institutions or the labor market (see Chapters 17 and 18) less tolerable than inequality that results from unequal efforts?

Second, if growing income inequality were always a bad thing, one should hope for stock market crashes. That's because the direct effects of such crashes hit the better-off disproportionately hard; income inequality, as it is usually measured, drops. Or take another example: Over the last 30 years there has been a strong trend toward two-income-earner households in the United States. Wives, especially those of well-to-do men, have entered the labor market. Those women work long hours, and usually earn high wages (see Chapter 11).[1] That alone contributes to inequality between households. Yet striving for equality clearly can't mean that well-qualified women ought to be discouraged from entering the labor force, or can it?

An increase (or decrease) in income inequality should therefore be judged by its causes. That's why it is important to look at what, besides more women in the workforce, has contributed to the rise in income inequality that the United States has witnessed over the last 30 or so years.

The Usual Suspects

Another possible cause for increasing inequality is the wave of immigration in recent decades. Because many immigrants are poorly educated, their presence in the labor market puts pressure on wages of less-skilled native workers. The erosion of the minimum wage may have added to that along with the decline of labor unions that had—as in Germany—always pushed for particularly high wage increases for the lowest income groups.[2]

Globalization, finally, might be another culprit. Increased competition from countries abundant with cheap labor may mean that low-skill jobs can be saved only if the wages for them grow less than average.[3]

But all those factors can't nearly explain the scope of unequal income distribution in America. Immigration and the erosion of the minimum wage may be important reasons for the unequal income distribution if the wage increases for low-skilled workers lag behind the increases for average-income earners; that, however, was not what happened. What happened was, as shown in Chapter 15, that high-income earners enjoyed far bigger income increases than average-income earners—a development that could not have been caused by immigration or a lowered minimum wage.

The suggestions set forth above are only partly plausible, anyway. The growth of income inequality started in the mid-1970s, that is, years before the erosion of the minimum wage and the decline of the unions began.[4] And if globalization is an essential factor, then one should expect inequality to increase most in countries that are particularly tightly knit into the global economy. But why then did inequality rise more pronouncedly in the United States than in Germany, whose imports relative to economic output are more than twice those of America?

It is therefore very likely that other causes are primarily responsible for the rise in income inequality.

The Great De(com)pression

As mentioned already, the well-to-do in America have enjoyed disproportionate gains in income over the last decades. Moreover, the people at the very top of the income scale benefited from the largest gains. The late Alfred Lerner, as CEO of MBNA, a credit card company, earned a staggering $194 million in 2002 alone.[5]

To get a more comprehensive impression, take a look at the share of the 10 and 1 percent of households that have the highest gross incomes (excluding capital gains). At the beginning of the 20th century, the top 10 percent in the United States accounted for more than 40 percent of all household incomes; the share of the top 1 percent alone was more than 15 percent. Then, very suddenly, came what is sometimes called "the great compression": the Great Depression and inflation, war and destruction, together with increasingly progressive taxation led to a significantly more equal distribution of incomes in the United States as well as other industrial countries such as France and the United Kingdom.[6]

In the 1970s and increasingly in the early 1980s, the share of top-income earners grew again in the United States. The years 1987 and 1988 saw especially high gains, perhaps as a result of the Reagan tax reform of 1986. At that time a dramatically lowered top marginal income tax rate might have led high-income earners to declare income that they had hitherto hidden from the IRS. However, in the following years the share of top-income earners grew more. Today, the situation in America looks similar to what it was before World War II.[7]

But who are these nouveaux riches in America? Where do their large income gains come from? How can those gains be reconciled with economic justice? Can society react? Should it?

Earned by Work

There were people who lived mostly on dividends and interest from their assets in 1929. Back then, more than 20 percent of the incomes of the richest 10 percent of American households was capital income. The top .5 percent earned 50 percent that way and the top ten-thousandth more than 70 percent. Today, on the other hand, even for the .01 percent at the top of the income ladder, capital income doesn't make up more than a seventh of income; the much larger remainder stems from salaries and entrepreneurial activities.[8]

Thus, high incomes in America are now largely earned by work. And, with few exceptions, inheritors are not at the top of the income earners. Rather, entrepreneurs, sports and entertainment stars, and top executives are the top income earners. Economist Robert Gordon calls them "the four Michaels"—a nod to computer entrepreneur Michael Dell, pop star Michael Jackson, basketball legend Michael Jordan, and Disney CEO Michael Eisner.[9]

Michael Dell represents the wave of corporate start-ups that began in the 1970s. Not even 20 years old and with—according to him—just $1,000 of capital, he founded the company that bears his name in 1984. His idea of selling computers straight from the manufacturer to the user turned out to be profitable. By 1992 his company had made it into the Fortune 500.[10]

This wave of new entrepreneurs is intimately connected to the revolution in information and communication technologies. Many founders of companies—Dell himself along with Microsoft's Bill Gates and Oracle's Larry Ellison—are themselves IT producers. Others were successful not least because they rigorously employed these technologies. Think of how the Walton family built up Wal-Mart (see Chapter 4).

Of course, some of those entrepreneurs—Gates and Ellison, for example—fought their way up with methods that could well be called ruthless. One could also argue that a somewhat higher taxation of their incomes would be appropriate. It is obvious nevertheless that American society has benefited tremendously from their restless efforts: they invented new technologies, helped people to make efficient use of them, and in the process created millions of new jobs.

Superstar Economics

The times in which a professional baseball player earned little more than an average American are long gone. Major league players have enjoyed dramatically rising incomes over the last decades. And they're not the only ones: that trend can be seen in all popular sports and in more or less the entire entertainment industry. Or, to be more precise, the incomes of stars rose to hitherto unheard of levels; the incomes of rank-and-file players and third-rate entertainers lagged behind.

That trend can be observed especially in the United States. When *Forbes* magazine ranks celebrities by their earning power (and media coverage), it finds that most of the top 100 celebrities worldwide are Americans or people who make their money mostly in the United States. Model Heidi Klum and racecar driver Michael Schumacher are the only Germans on that list.[11]

That development, too, was assisted by technological progress. The late economist Sherwin Rosen said as much in a paper over 20 years ago.[12] There used to be, Rosen argued, lots of comedians in the United States, each of whom made a rather modest income performing in front of live audiences. Nowadays, however, the market is dominated by a handful of comedians who enjoy superstar status.

Rosen saw one cause for those changes in technological advances like television.[13] While performances of singers, actors, and sport

stars in the past could be watched only by physically present specta-
tors, TV and satellites made it possible to broadcast the pictures all
over the country and shortly thereafter over the entire globe.

The larger the market sport stars and entertainers can reach, the
greater the demand for the best of them will be. That is because
experience teaches that people are willing to pay a considerable
premium to see a Michael Jordan, a Tiger Woods, or a David Beck-
ham—even when those superstars may objectively be just marginally better than the people in the second or third tier. That is, according to Rosen's theory, the reason why technological progress helped
superstars, relative to their colleagues and the rest of the population,
to experience such huge gains in income.

It's also one of the reasons why the phenomenon is most pronounced in America. The European equivalents to David Letterman
and Jay Leno serve much smaller markets; their domestic audience
is smaller, as is their international fan base, simply because German
and Italian are not exactly lingua francas. David Letterman is well-
known in Germany, but who in America (or France or Italy for that
matter) has ever heard of his German counterpart, Harald Schmidt?

In the end, rising incomes of superstars reflect a rise in demand
for their talents, just as the riches of Michael Dell and other entrepreneurs are based on a large demand for their products. There isn't
anything indecent about it. Why shouldn't Roger Clemens sell his
services to the baseball franchise that offers him the most attractive
salary? Just as with companies, the question is only whether or not
a society wants to limit the income of superstars with a progressive
tax system.

Gilt Wastebaskets

In June 2003 Johannes Rau, the Social Democrat who was serving
as president of Germany at the time, called for "smaller differences
between the incomes of a blue-collar worker and a manager"—the
reason being that "we mustn't slip down into American conditions."[14]

Actually, when it comes to executive pay, there are already "American conditions" in Germany. Or sort of. CEO salaries in absolute
terms are significantly lower than in the United States, but German
executives head companies that tend to be either smaller or less
profitable, or both. In 2002 their executive boards cost the 30 largest
publicly listed companies an average of .12 percent of profits; for

comparison, the top echelons of the 30 companies listed in the Dow Jones Industrial Average index cost their shareholders .08 percent.[15]

Nevertheless, it can't be denied that executive compensation has, in many cases, grown out of control in the United States. For instance, Richard Brown, who was removed as CEO of Electronic Data Systems in March 2003, collected $37 million in severance. A little earlier, Brown had directed that severance pay for thousands of fired EDS employees be cut from a maximum of 26 weeks to 4.[16]

Dennis Kozlowski pushed the envelope even further. Allegedly, the former CEO of Tyco had his employer pay for a fitness coach for his wife. It is also said that he billed Tyco $97,000 for flowers, $72,000 for jewelry, $6,000 for a shower curtain, and $2,200 for a gilt wastebasket. Prosecutors accuse him and his former chief financial officer Mark Swartz of stealing almost $600 million in unauthorized compensation and illicit stock sales.[17]

That mentality of reckless self-enrichment, however, is found in European countries such as Germany as well. The management board of BASF got a raise of 46 percent in 2002, a year in which both the stock price of the German chemicals manufacturer and its revenue fell. Also in 2002, the top executives of German semiconductor producer Infineon Technologies helped themselves to a 33 percent increase in pay. That the company declared a net loss of several billions that year apparently didn't matter very much.

Sexual Revolution in the Executive Suite

Where do those flashes of "infectious greed," as Fed chairman Alan Greenspan dubbed the phenomenon, come from? How can it be that men like Dennis Koslowski rule companies like latter-day Sun Kings, obviously failing to recognize that their personal interest is not identical with the interest of the companies they serve?

A popular explanation is that social norms have been blurred. Princeton economist Paul Krugman, for instance, points out:

> For a generation after World War II, fear of outrage kept executive salaries in check. Now the outrage is gone. That is, the explosion of executive pay represents a social change rather than the purely economic forces of supply and demand. We should think of it not as a market trend like the rising value of waterfront property but as something more like the sexual revolution of the 1960's—a relaxation of old strictures, a new permissiveness. . . .[18]

But executives can satisfy their greed only if there is someone who allows this "new permissiveness," the shareholder. She, after all, is the employer of the executives and the CEOs salaries come from her pockets.

How could the present situation have developed without shareholders taking action? One possibility is very simply that the owners were guileless. That's understandable insofar as many executives have not given their shareholders much cause for complaint in the last two decades. Even after a three-year bear market, the Dow Jones in the spring of 2003 was nominally still at 10 times the low levels it hit in 1982.

Closely related to that is the spillover of the superstar phenomenon into the corporate world. When the then-CEO of Chrysler Lee Iacocca turned up on magazine covers in the early 1980s, that was a novelty. Since the 1990s, at the latest, it's a routine occurrence. Many CEOs thus became famous. Almost magical abilities were attributed to some—former General Electric CEO Jack Welsh, for example. In such an environment it is only to be expected that superstar CEOs are doused with money, even if a less well-known manager would do as good a job for a tenth of the salary.[19]

Finally, it was overlooked that during the stock market boom shareholders had only limited control over executives. For years it went unnoticed that well-known companies like Adelphia, Enron, Global Crossing, and Worldcom were cooking their books. And when Tyco sold its subsidiary ADT Automotive, Kozlowski's top managers congratulated themselves with bonuses totaling $56 million. The shareholders were not informed. On the contrary, all beneficiaries were forbidden to talk about the matter. In Tyco's accounting records, the bonuses were hidden as "direct selling costs."[20]

What to Do?

Lawmakers on both sides of the Atlantic would be well-advised to look for a new regulatory framework that allows shareholders better control of managements. Especially more stringent disclosure requirements would seem useful. But no Congress or administration can exercise that control itself. Regulations of any kind seem likely to remain ineffective if those whose money is involved, namely shareholders, don't look out.

But what else could lawmakers do to keep executive pay within a range considered reasonable by the public and the shareholders? Appeals to modesty, like President Rau's, are certainly one possibility. Another would be, again, higher taxes.

However, insofar as lack of effective control on the part of shareholders is the basis for a grab-all mentality among executives, neither emotional appeals nor higher taxes will be able to do much. If lack of control is the problem, more taxes would only lead to managers paying themselves higher gross salaries so as not to take any cut in net pay.

The United States has had experience with this. Congress has tried numerous times to rein in the compensation of top managers. But the CEOs have so far always found a way to circumvent new regulations. Sometimes new laws even turned out to be counterproductive. One example is a piece of 1993 legislation in which Congress increased the tax liabilities for salaries in excess of $1 million. That gave companies an incentive to choose stock options as the preferred form of compensation and was one of the reasons for the stock option mania of the late 1990s.[21]

Should Michael Dell Have Become a Teacher?

According to *Forbes,* the average wealth of the 400 richest people in America was $2.15 billion in 2001—less than in 2000, at the height of the stock market boom, when the average reached $3.06 billion. But it was still more than twice their average worth in 1989 ($.92 billion).[22]

That list of the superrich has seen names come and go: 230 of the 400 people in the *Forbes* ranking of 2001 cannot be found on the list from 1989. Of the 230 newcomers, 210 achieved their ranking through their own work; in only about 20 cases was inheritance the cause.[23]

However, given such huge amounts of wealth as were created over the last two decades, it seems more and more likely that the rich of tomorrow will be the children of today's rich. In 2001 about one-third of all private wealth was already in the hands of the richest 1 percent of the population; the next 9 percent owned another third. The final third was shared by the remaining 90 percent of the population.[24] That already high concentration seems likely to increase further; America may witness the revival of a class of people who receive riches from their folks rather than their own efforts.

Such a trend would be difficult to reconcile with the much-lauded American ideal of a "meritocracy," according to which individual achievement is supposed to be the determining factor for personal success and wealth. From that perspective, the creation of a new class of superrich is certainly a concern.

Still, ridiculously high salaries for executives in the United States have nothing to do with the fact that America's brand of capitalism is rather unrestrained. At their core those salaries are a reflection of weakness in the corporate governance system, in the ability of owners to direct the actions of their employees. That weakness is anything but an inherent part of the American economic model.[25]

As for entrepreneurs, it can be assumed that most founders are driven not by some noble ideal but rather by the simple wish to become rich—filthy rich to be precise. That's the reason why a society that is concerned about its own well-being has to assess whether it might not be better, for all the dangers to the meritocracy ideal, to accept the possibility of successful entrepreneurs amassing gargantuan riches.

Put differently: The income distribution in the United States would surely be more even if the Waltons had remained grocers, if the Dells had become high school teachers, and if the Ellisons had become journalists. If income inequality is the yardstick, America would be a more "just" country today—but almost certainly a poorer one, too.

Rewards for Education

The "four Michaels" explain part of the unique increase in income inequality in the United States. There is a broad consensus among economists, however, that another factor played a more crucial role: technological progress.[26]

Sometimes, technological progress leads to the replacement of high-skill employees with cheap, untrained labor. The classic example is industrialization in the 19th century. In the newly erected factories, labor was, initially at any rate, less demanding than in the manufactures that they replaced. In such cases, progress has the tendency to lessen income inequalities.

Technological progress in industrial countries since the beginning of the 20th century, however, has been of a different kind. It makes necessary an increasingly higher share of qualified workers. The production of microchips, after all, demands a more skilled work-force than running a steel mill.[27]

There is wide consensus among economists, too, that that long-term trend has only strengthened over the last decades. Statistics back up that claim. In 1900 only 1 in 10 workers in the United States was in a professional, technical, or managerial position. In 1970 that share was 2 in 10. Today, not even 35 years later, about a third of the American workforce holds those kinds of positions.[28]

When the forces of the market are allowed to operate and, for example, the demand rises for a constant supply of bicycles, produc-ers can ask higher prices. The same principle applies on the labor market. When the demand for highly skilled labor increases while only a fixed number of such workers are available, it's only logical that the income of the highly skilled will rise more quickly than the wages of less-qualified workers.

Precisely that can be observed in the United States. Empirical studies have found that those sectors of the economy that invest most in high tech have the highest demand for highly qualified workers and pay them, relative to low-skilled workers, the highest wages.[29] The so-called college premium has accordingly been on the rise. In 1975 college graduates commanded incomes than were on average 57 percent higher than the incomes of those who had only graduated from high school. In 2001 that premium stood at 89 per-cent (Figure 16.1). The relative rise was even more pronounced among workers who had a master's or other advanced degree.

How should we judge that considerable college premium and its rise over time? Should politics counter the trend and, if so, what would be the consequences?

Increasing premiums for education are nothing new. In the early 20th century the same thing happened in America among workers in manufacturing. Back then, technological progress made it important that workers had not only two strong hands but also cognitive abilities, such as reading, for understanding manuals, blueprints, and formulas. The result was a wage increase for workers with a high school diploma. Enrollment in high schools promptly rose significantly in the 1920s and 1930s.[30]

The example suggests that, in a market economy, prices, including wages and salaries, reflect more than just shortages; they also are signals to existing producers to increase their output and to newcom-ers to enter the market. That mechanism works on the labor market

Figure 16.1
COLLEGE PREMIUM IN THE UNITED STATES
(MEAN ANNUAL INCOME BY EDUCATIONAL ATTAINMENT AS
PERCENT OF MEAN INCOME OF HIGH SCHOOL GRADUATES)

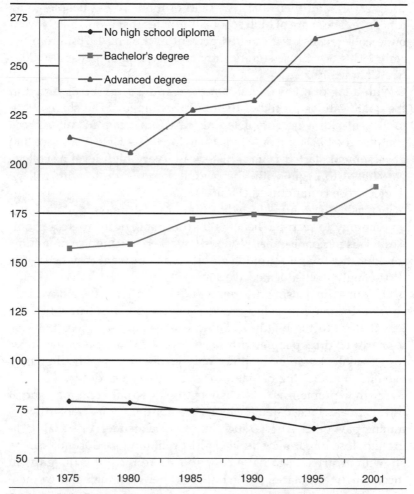

SOURCES: U.S. Census Bureau (www.census.gov) and author's calculations.

as well, as long as wages are entrusted to the forces of supply and demand. An increasing demand for qualified workers will lead to higher wages for those employees, which will in turn induce them

165

to work more and lead a greater share of the young generation to seek higher skills.

Both effects have been seen in the United States since the 1970s. There's increased participation of women in the workforce (see Chapter 11), and there's also a trend of more young people going to college. The share of high school graduates that immediately went on to college was at around 50 percent in the late 1970s. From the early 1980s on, it rose significantly and reached 65 percent in 2002 (see Chapter 19).[31]

With a lag of a few years, that development can be observed in the qualifications profile of the adult population. The share of 25- to 29-year-olds who completed at least four years of college rose gently in the 1980s and only took off in the 1990s. However, since that development started from a historically very high level of college enrollment to begin with, the overall share of those with college degrees rose continuously (Figure 16.2).

Increasing premiums for education are instrumental in enabling an economy to reap the benefits that technological progress promises.[32] This mechanism has obviously worked in America: premiums for education help to provide employers with what they need—an increasingly well-educated workforce.

Of course, increasing returns on education have their downside as well. Income inequality grows. That's especially true when the jobs that go to the highly skilled are not really new jobs but jobs formerly held by people with fewer skills. In that case, the wages for less-skilled workers will not only grow more slowly; they may even fall, because the demand for such labor goes down.

Yet that problem is less challenging to social cohesion than it might appear. First, if qualifications become more important in determining pay, other criteria, such like as race, gender, or social background, lose importance. Indeed, the premium for education can be shown empirically to have contributed to bridging the gaps in income between blacks and whites and between men and women. Thus, the education premium increased one type of inequality and also helped reduce another, doubtlessly more problematic, one.[33]

What's more, an increasing college premium is not necessarily a permanent phenomenon. When demand outstrips supply on the bicycle market, prices will rise—but only until an increase of production has brought supply in line with demand again.

Figure 16.2
SHARE OF COLLEGE GRADUATES IN THE UNITED STATES
(PERSONS WHO COMPLETED FOUR YEARS OF COLLEGE OR MORE AS A
PERCENT OF THE NONINSTITUTIONAL POPULATION)

SOURCE: U.S. Census Bureau (www.census.gov).

Such balancing will take much longer on the labor market, not least because it takes more time to produce a larger number of college graduates.[34] And, unlike the bicycle example, it is not to be expected that the college premium will fall back to its original level. Neither are there any indications that technological progress will not further increase the demand for highly skilled workers, nor can the share of college graduates be increased indefinitely. Even in an optimal education system, not every high school graduate will be able to succeed in college.[35]

167

Still, American economists of all political leanings agree that although the college premium might remain large in the United States, it won't remain as large as it is today.[36]

The Price of Equality

In the United States a significantly larger part of the population has attained a high-quality education than in France, Germany, or Italy. And, with the exception of France, that difference has been increasing in recent years.

According to OECD statistics, the share of 25- to 34-year-old Americans who had completed an education at the tertiary level rose from 30 to 39 percent between 1991 and 2001. Germany saw only an increase from 20 to 21 percent. In Italy the increase amounted to five percentage points—but at 12 percent, the share was still very small in 2001.[37]

In France, during the same period, that share grew by an impressive 14 percentage points from 20 to 34 percent. No further increases, however, can be expected in the near future, as France was one of the two OECD countries in which total tertiary enrollment was lower in 2001 than in 1995.[38] (Germany was the other.)

Of course, the fact that the United States does not have an expanded system of vocational training and therefore provides high school graduates with few alternatives to a college education is one reason for the greater percentage of Americans with tertiary educations. Another reason, though, is likely to be the lower college premium in Europe (Figure 16.3). Indeed, the premium is so much lower that one can assume it to be one of the main reasons for the transatlantic differences in income distribution.

Even if you consider the much higher tuition fees in the United States (see Chapter 18), going to college remains a much more profitable investment for Americans than for continental Europeans. That is shown by the annual return that college graduates receive in the form of higher wages and greater job security.

The OECD puts that return at 19.6 percent for men in the United States in 1999–2000. For men in France (13.0 percent), Germany (9.3 percent), and Italy (7.2 percent), the payoff was much smaller. For women the transatlantic difference is even a bit larger. True, if tuition fees are taken into account, the return declines by 4.7 percentage points in the United States and only by between .3 and .8 percentage

Figure 16.3
COLLEGE PREMIUM IN THE UNITED STATES, FRANCE, ITALY, AND GERMANY
(MEAN INCOME BEFORE TAXES OF PERSONS WITH COMPLETED TERTIARY EDUCATION IN PERCENT OF INCOMES OF PERSONS WITH COMPLETED UPPER SECONDARY EDUCATION, 25- TO 64-YEAR-OLDS)

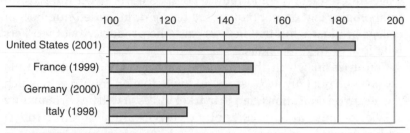

SOURCE: OECD (2003d), p. 165.

point in the three European countries. But even then, the difference remains considerable. In Italy the net return is not even half as great as it is in the United States.[39]

How that discrepancy came about is difficult to say. It is of course possible that the smaller premium in the European countries is the unintended side effect of political decisions and institutional arrangements. It is, however, equally possible that the small returns reflect a deliberate decision to keep income inequality ')w.[40]

Whether intentionally or not, premiums for education are artificially lowered when unions succeed in preventing wage differentiation. The premiums are further dampened by anything that diminishes the demand for highly qualified workers, including strict employment protection legislation that keeps companies from replacing jobs of low-skill workers with jobs for high-skilled workers. Everything that impedes structural change, such as strict regulation of start-up companies, belongs in the same category (see Chapter 4).

The consequence of an artificially reduced college premium is quite obvious: New technologies will be implemented at a slower pace. That's exactly what happened in France, Germany, and Italy where investments in information and communication technologies are far smaller than in the United States (see Chapter 3). The potential productivity growth that those technologies promise is thus realized only after a time lag. Per capita income grows more slowly than it could but will, in the end, reach the same level as in countries that adapt more quickly.

Maybe, however, the path of adjustment will look altogether different. A combination of rigid employment protection laws and little wage differentiation could induce companies to invest foremost in technologies that do not require the hiring of increased numbers of college graduates but that instead raise the productivity of workers with low or medium skills.[41]

Countries in which that happens pay a high price: Per capita income will not only increase more slowly than in countries in which the return on education is left to market forces; it will be permanently smaller because the capacities of the citizens are not used to fullest advantage.

That this is what actually happens in France, Germany, or Italy cannot be proven here. But in Germany, at least, there is a strong indication that it might be the case. Although in Germany the share of college graduates is significantly smaller than in the United States (and many other industrial countries), one hardly ever hears employers complain about a lack of college graduates on the labor market. What has established itself as a code word in the German economic policy debate, however, is *Facharbeitermangel*, a lack of trained blue-collar workers.

Youth Craze? What Youth Craze?

The discussion so far has much simplified reality. Not only technological progress but also the transition to a service economy and the repudiation of Taylorism have likely contributed to a disproportionate increase in demand for highly qualified workers (see Chapter 4).

Similarly, qualification can't simply be equated with formal education. Not only the diploma counts, but also the chosen academic subjects, computer skills, skills gained "on the job," and "soft skills" such the ability to work in teams.[42]

All of the factors are, in one way or another, linked to a phenomenon that, in analogy to the college premium, could be called an "experience premium." To be sure, the media often pronounce that there is a youth craze in companies these days. The accusation seems to make sense: If it's true that technological progress makes knowledge and skills become outdated more quickly, young graduates

Figure 16.4
THE "EXPERIENCE PREMIUM" IN THE UNITED STATES
(MEDIAN WEEKLY EARNINGS OF FULL-TIME WAGE AND SALARY
WORKERS BY AGE; MEDIAN EARNINGS
OF 16- TO 24-YEAR-OLDS = 100)

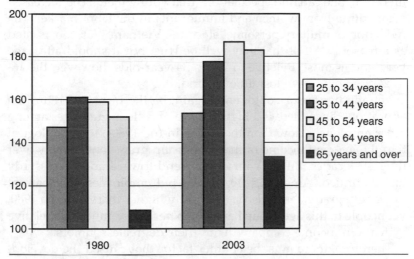

SOURCES: BLS and author's calculations.

should receive relatively higher incomes for their fresh and up-to-date education than used to be the case. One would expect that to be especially true today, when for the first time a generation that grew up in front of PCs has hit the labor market.

But even if there is a youth craze in hiring, it can't be detected in American earning statistics. The opposite, if anything, is true. Among full-time wage and salary workers in the United States in 1980, 35- to 44-year-old employees made the highest incomes (Figure 16.4). Today, 45- to 54-year-olds are the age group with the highest earnings, followed by the 55- to 64-year-olds.

That continues a trend that has existed in the United States at least since the 1970s. It can be seen in many other OECD countries as well, though it is nowhere as pronounced as in the United States.[43]

That development brought with it increased income inequality, because the best earning age groups are further ahead now than they were some 20 years ago. The average worker between ages 45

171

and 54 earned 59 percent more than the average 16- to 24-year-old in 1980; by 2003 that gap had widened to 87 percent. Herein, in other words, lies another reason for the increase in income inequality over the last decades.

The causes of this development are not known. In the economic literature, one can find speculations that young men faced increased competition from women and immigrants in the labor market. The reduction of military personnel since the Vietnam War, too, is cited as a reason.[44] All of that may well be true, but it should affect the very young most. Relative to 25- to 34-year-olds, however, the 16- to 24-year-olds have lost little ground.

Yet another factor could, once again, be the increased return on education. Since there is a higher share of college graduates among older employees now than there was in the 1980s, it's only logical that the average income of that age group grew considerably over the last decades. But, of course, the trend toward additional study has continued. Among 25- to 34-year-old employees, the share of university graduates is also significantly higher than it was in 1980, yet people in this age group have not experienced much of a relative increase in income compared with their degreeless juniors.

Therefore, there must be another factor that caused the development shown in Figure 16.4. Something must have happened that favored older workers especially—indeed, so much so that it over-compensated for the presumed youth craze.

Perhaps that factor is simply the fact that experience on the job is worth more to an employer than it used to be. A historical comparison makes that explanation seem quite plausible. In an agrarian society, the average worker is a farmer whose productivity decreases with age. In an industrial society, the importance of physical ability and stamina declines, and in a service society it becomes negligible. Meanwhile, experience and the knowledge connected with it become more important.

What is relevant here, however, is not so much the cause of the phenomenon but its meaning for income distribution and for the assessment of its development. Insofar as the increase in income inequality can be attributed to a widening income discrepancy between young and old, it isn't quite as worrying. That's because, in this case, the usual indicators, reflecting *annual* incomes, record a growing inequality, but the distribution of *lifetime* incomes doesn't change at all.

* * *

Inequality doesn't equal injustice. When inequality in the distribution of income increases because income is increasingly dependent on experience and therefore age, it is difficult to see what's so unfair—after all, (almost) everyone grows old.

High premiums on education, on the other hand, might be considered undesirable if one's concern is equality of distribution. But at least inequality based on educational achievement is less problematic than other kinds of inequality. That's particularly the case when it pushes back discrimination based on factors such as race or gender.

Furthermore, the college premium is instrumental in an economy's adjustment to technological progress. Once the adjustment is made, the premium declines. Such adjustments are just that—adjustments.

Finally, the less political or institutional meddling disturbs rises and falls of the college premium, the faster it will fulfill its function and return to its longer-term level. It would therefore not be surprising if the coming decades saw the inequality of incomes recede again in the United States while it continued to rise in France, Germany, and Italy.

17. Mass Unemployment—The Mother of All Injustices

To be unemployed is a heavy lot. That has not been lost on Germany's federal government, which currently presides over mass unemployment that directly affects six million people, the largest number since the early 1930s when the Great Depression helped to sweep Adolf Hitler into power.

The ruling coalition of Social Democrats and Greens describes the consequences of unemployment on the affected individual in its 2001 "Report on Poverty and Wealth": "Depressive moods, general dissatisfaction with life, fear, helplessness and hopelessness, low self-esteem, resignation bordering on apathy, a low level of activity, social isolation and loneliness represent the most important symptoms." That "physical symptoms manifest themselves only after some time" is not much consolation.[1]

If unemployment means suffering, mass unemployment means suffering on a massive scale. And of course, full employment has tremendous benefits. For one, unemployment is a fiscal double whammy. With every additional unemployed person, there is not only one more benefit recipient but also one fewer taxpayer. Thus, high unemployment can create a vicious cycle: It tends to increase the burden on those still employed, which weakens incentives. That, in turn, can hamper economic growth and job creation, thereby deepening the labor market crisis. A high level of employment, on the other hand, is an easy way to ensure that the tax burden remains within reasonable bounds.

In addition, full employment means that workers can benefit from advances in productivity, as happened in the U.S. economy in the late 1990s when workers received increased pay without negative effects for the labor market (see Chapter 3).[2]

Finally—and most important from a social policy perspective—low unemployment particularly helps workers with low qualifications or little work experience, in other words, the very people who

175

Figure 17.1
DECLINE OF UNEMPLOYMENT RATES IN THE UNITED STATES
(SELECTED DEMOGRAPHIC GROUPS, PERCENTAGE POINTS, SEASONALLY ADJUSTED DATA)

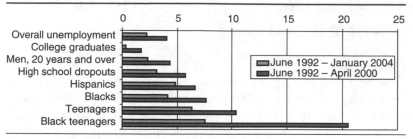

SOURCES: BLS (www.bls.gov) and author's calculations.

have faced the gravest problems on the labor markets of industrialized countries in the last couple of decades.

Small Difference, Big Effect

Especially in times when technological progress greatly benefits highly qualified workers, it's difficult to integrate unskilled laborers. They tend to get an opportunity only when no highly qualified workers can be found on the job market. Only then are employers willing to lower the demands on new workers and to offer the necessary training.

That was exactly what happened during the U.S. boom of the 1990s.[3] The already low unemployment among college graduates sank further and further during that time—at one point down to 1.5 percent. Thus, the labor market was indeed virtually depleted of highly qualified workers. Opportunities were then made available to the disadvantaged—ethnic minorities, teenagers, and high school dropouts. At the height of the boom, employers were outright desperate. A restaurant in Atlanta advertised: "Now hiring. Must have a pulse."[4]

In the wake of the 2001 recession, the gains of the 1990s partly evaporated, but the crisis did not eliminate them. In January 2004 the unemployment rate among disadvantaged groups was still considerably lower than it had been when the overall unemployment rate reached its last cyclical peak in June 1992 (Figure 17.1).

176

Economist Paul Krugman summarizes this phenomenon in the following way:

> A tight labor market disproportionately benefits marginal workers, those who tend to be the last hired, first fired; for those attempting to take the first step out of the underclass the difference between 6 percent and 5 percent unemployment may be a large difference indeed.[5]

If one percentage point—the difference between 6 and 5 percent—can make such a difference, just imagine what the effect would be on France, Germany, and Italy if unemployment there could be reduced from 10 or 12 percent to 6 percent!

Long-Term Unemployment: The Really Big Scandal

High unemployment in many parts of continental Europe is bad enough as it is. What makes it a true social catastrophe is the fact that more and more people are permanently excluded from gainful employment.

Not only are relatively more people jobless in France, Germany, and Italy than in the United States, they're without jobs for much longer. To be sure, in the United States the rise in long-term unemployment in the early years of the current decade drew a lot of media attention. And indeed, according to the OECD, the share of unemployed people in the United States who found new jobs only after more than six months stood at 11.4 percent in 2000, the last year of the record-breaking boom of the 1990s. Just two years later, in 2002, that number had risen to 18.3 percent.[6]

For now, however, these numbers are not exceptionally high compared with those from recent U.S. history. After the preceding two recessions, the incidence of long-term unemployment was higher in the United States. In 1983 long-term unemployment, defined as the share of people who remained unemployed for more than six months, reached a cyclical peak at 23.9 percent; in 1992 long-term unemployment peaked at 20.3 percent.[7]

Elsewhere, the picture is much bleaker anyway: As early as the late 1970s long-term unemployment in Germany and other European countries increased markedly—a strong indication that the performance of the labor market even at that time, if compared with that of the United States, wasn't as good as a simple look at overall unemployment rates might suggest (see Chapter 2).

177

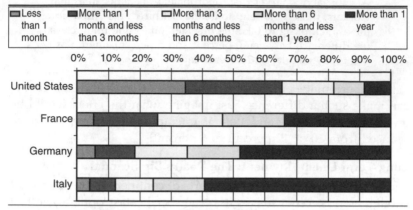

Figure 17.2
DURATION OF UNEMPLOYMENT SPELLS
(% OF TOTAL UNEMPLOYMENT, 2002)

SOURCE: OECD (2003b), pp. 75, 171, 181, 231.

In the decades since, more and more people have lost their jobs during recessions and failed to find new work as economies cyclically improved.[8] As a result, for the past 10 years, approximately two of three unemployed people in Germany have needed more than six months to find a new job. In Italy, three of four unemployed people remain shut out of the labor market for that long (Figure 17.2).

Long-term unemployment excludes a large share of the affected people from all the benefits that go along with work, such as prosperity, self-respect, and the respect of others. Economists speak in such cases of "hysteresis"—the ongoing existence of a condition independent of the forces by which it was initially caused. That is because the longer unemployment lasts, the more difficult it is to reenter the workforce: As pointed out already, in times of rapid technological progress, acquired skills become obsolete more quickly. And after a while, even skills that are natural to others begin to suffer. In the wake of welfare reform in the United States it became obvious that the long-term unemployed must often be trained to do even simple tasks. For example, many of the people affected found it difficult to live by the clock again and to keep appointments.[9]

In addition, longtime unemployment tends to deepen already existing labor market problems further. If many people are unemployed for a long time and have either given up looking for work or are of only limited employability because of eroded skills, that might reduce downward pressures on wages that could otherwise induce employers to hire more workers. In such a case, only a continuously rising unemployment rate can ensure that pressures on wages persist.[10]

As Egalitarian As It Gets

Mass unemployment, especially when it goes hand in hand with long-term unemployment, is a phenomenon that can't be reconciled with economic or social justice, however defined. In that light, Nobel prize–winning economist Joseph Stiglitz denies that the often assumed tension between economic growth and employment on the one side and economic justice and security on the other even exists:

> There is no such trade-off. The worst thing for most people is not to have a job. To marginalize people and to label them unproductive members of society has devastating economic and social consequences. Therefore, one of the great successes of the U.S. economy in the past few years was to bring down the unemployment rate to five percent. It gave formerly marginalized people new opportunities. That's as egalitarian as it gets.[11]

18. Inequality in Education—The Grandmother of All Injustices

You can't say it any better than German chancellor Gerhard Schröder did: "The access to education and the quality of our education system—that is the social question of the dawning 21st century. Access to education always means access to a decent life."[1]

If that's the measuring stick, America is in trouble—with regard to higher education and even more so with regard to the public school system. It may be true that a lack of accountability and competition is to blame for failing inner-city schools; it may also be true that underfunding of public schools in low-income districts is the main problem and that greater spending on schools would be beneficial to American society as a whole.

What is definitely *not* true, however, is that public spending on schools is unusually low in the United States. In 2000 expenditures on education amounted to 3.5 percent of GDP. The French government spends more (4.0 percent). However, the levels of public spending on education are lower in Italy (3.2 percent), Germany (2.9 percent), and for the OECD on average (3.3 percent).[2]

A Humiliation Named Pisa

What's also *not* true is that American schools perform dismally compared to French, Italian, and particularly German schools. The OECD's "Pisa" study demonstrated as much.

"Pisa" examined the performance of 15-year-old students in 28 industrialized countries as well as Brazil, Latvia, Luxembourg, and Russia. Here are some of its findings:[3]

- With a study-wide average of 500 points for the reading skills of students, Germans received 484, Italians 487, Americans 504, and the French 505 points.
- In no other OECD country was the difference between the worst and the best students in reading proficiency bigger than in

Germany, and the best German readers weren't even particularly good in international comparison.

- The share of students that had very good reading skills (level 5) was bigger in the United States than in France, Germany, and Italy.
- The share of students that could read only at the most elementary level was greater in the United States than in France but smaller than in Italy and much smaller than in Germany.
- The picture was similar with regard to math skills. The United States ranked below the OECD average but was still ahead of Germany and Italy. The gap between the worst and the best students here, too, was smaller in America than in Germany.

Equally depressing from a German point of view was that, according to Pisa, reading skills of German students depend more on the socioeconomic status of their parents than do those of students in any other OECD country. Thus, an analysis of the Pisa results by the Max-Planck-Institut für Bildungsforschung, a renowned public research institution in Berlin, concluded, "Even the United States, so often singled out as an example of big social disparities in educational opportunities, displays considerable but still significantly lower socially caused skill differences" than Germany.[4] What's more, over the last decades the correlation between skills and family background in Germany actually increased.[5]

The causes of this situation are not going to be speculated about here. But it should be noted that if the chancellor is measured by his own words, he governs a country that has a very unjust school system—at least compared with the American system.

That impression is only furthered when one takes a look at the university system.

You Get What You Pay for

It's been a long time since Heidelberg outshone Harvard. It's also been a long time since world-class research at German universities was more than an exception. And it's been a long time since most German Nobel laureates actually conducted their research in their home country (rather than in the United States).

One obvious reason for that decline was the emigration of countless top scientists during the Nazi regime. But there's another likely reason: in 2000 Germans spent a mere 1.0 percent of their GDP on

Figure 18.1
EXPENDITURES ON TERTIARY EDUCATIONAL INSTITUTIONS IN THE
UNITED STATES, FRANCE, GERMANY, AND ITALY
(AS A PERCENTAGE OF GDP, 2000)

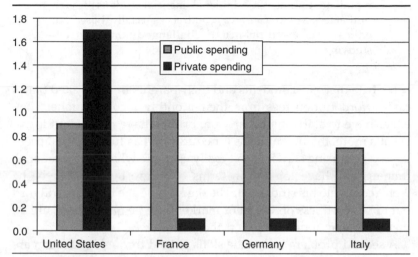

SOURCE: OECD (2003d), p. 208.

their university system. The French (1.1 percent) and Italians (0.9 percent) spent about the same amount. To the Americans, on the other hand, colleges and universities were worth a much higher share, 2.7 percent (Figure 18.1).

The difference is similarly large when expenditures for academic research are excluded and only core educational services are considered. Adjusted for purchasing power parities, Germany spent $6,643 per student for those services at the tertiary level in 2000; Italy spent $7,717 and France $6,094. Compare that to the United States, which spent $16,982.[6]

The reason for the discrepancy is easily found: Almost two-thirds of the expenditures for tertiary educational institutions are financed privately in the United States, mostly through tuition fees. The private sectors in France, Germany, and Italy, on the other hand, spend no more than .1 percent of GDP for tertiary education.

In Europe, asking students and their parents to contribute any more is usually considered incompatible with the welfare state's aim of providing equal opportunity for everyone. The German government, for example, states:

> To ensure equal opportunities, the federal government repudiates tuition fees. Additional financial burdens through tuition fees would scare away children, especially those from educationally and financially challenged families, from studying.[7]

It's true that most students and their parents in the United States can't afford tuition fees from their monthly incomes alone. They either have to start saving early on, or they have to take out loans. What's more, taking out loans for education has fundamental problems. An aspiring student can't easily estimate what value academic training will have for him in terms of future income. Maybe he won't complete his studies; maybe the knowledge he gains will turn out to be worthless on the labor market once he graduates. Tuition, therefore, may indeed scare off the risk averse.

A second problem is that the skills gained through education are not liquid assets. Buying a house gives you the option to sell if you can't make the mortgage payments anymore. And your bank can hold the house as collateral. A student, on the other hand, can't (and shouldn't be able to) sell himself or offer himself as collateral.[8]

Those problems are not solved optimally in the United States. Student loans, given out by colleges and the government, don't cover the entire cost. The creditors offer only a limited amount of money since the loan guarantees and interest rate reductions that come with these loans amount to a costly subsidy. Thus, when tuition fees for colleges rose sharply in the 1980s and 1990s, it became increasingly difficult to get the money necessary for an education.

If that trend continues, American politicians might sooner or later look to alternative forms of financing in order to continue to ensure that children from poor families have access to a university education. One possibility would be loan contracts according to which the student would pay back, not a predetermined *amount* after leaving college, but rather a predetermined *percentage* of her income. Such an arrangement could make handing out student loans a profitable undertaking, thereby increasing supply. It would also allow students to take out larger loans without risking being buried in debt.[9]

Figure 18.2
COLLEGE ENROLLMENT IN THE UNITED STATES
(PERCENTAGE OF HIGH SCHOOL COMPLETERS WHO WERE ENROLLED
IN COLLEGE THE OCTOBER AFTER COMPLETING HIGH SCHOOL)

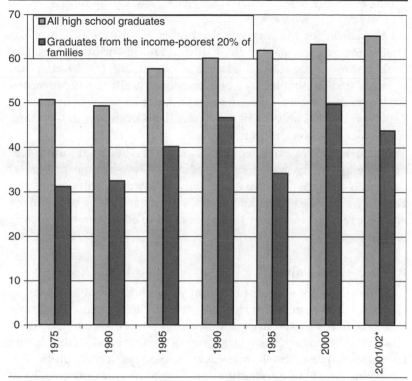

SOURCES: BLS (www.bls.gov); and U.S. Department of Education (2003), p. 127.

Until now, however, the current system of financing has worked reasonably well, at least in comparison with other countries' systems. It enables a significant and rising share of young Americans to have access to a college education. Take, for instance, students who completed high school in 2002: 43.8 percent of those who came from the fifth of households that had the lowest family income were enrolled in college the following October (Figure 18.2).

That means that the likelihood that the poorest American youth will attend college is, on average, greater than the likelihood that

German youth from *average*-income families will do so. Or, to use a different indicator, in 2001 a 17-year-old in the United States could statistically expect to receive 3.5 years of tertiary education. The only industrialized country where this number is higher is Finland (4.2 years); France (2.6 years), Italy (2.4 years), and Germany (2.1 years) do considerably worse.[10]

One reason for that may be the higher college premium in the United States (see Chapter 16). Cultural and historical factors, too, could be among the reasons. Many authors, among them Karl Marx, have pointed out that the lack of a feudalistic heritage has prevented the emergence of class consciousness in America.[11] Not so in Europe. Tellingly, in 2000 only 13 percent of college freshmen in Germany were working-class children.[12]

Whatever the reason, it seems obvious that while high tuition fees do have a negative effect on the share of low-income groups at American colleges and universities, much lower fees in continental Europe haven't led to better results. A country like Germany does *not* achieve a greater degree of equal access to education by rejecting tuition fees.

It's Free—And Unjust

Tuition fees are still an exception in Germany, but studying in Germany is, of course, not free. It's free only in the sense that those who benefit from a tertiary education don't pick up the bill. Instead, blue-collar taxpayers bear a large part of the cost of educating future lawyers and engineers. In other words, the rejection of tuition fees is nothing less than a redistribution of income from the bottom to the top.[13]

Economist Karl-Dieter Grüske did the most comprehensive analysis of those redistribution effects in Germany. His study is already 10 years old, but because no significant reforms have since taken place, its results can be assumed to still be at least roughly valid.

Grüske found that low-income households that send children to college profit the most from the German system of financing tertiary education. Their benefits in the form of educational services and direct education-related transfer payments outweigh their contribution through taxes by a factor of 50. Given the progressive tax code, the cost/benefit ratio for high-income families is certainly less favorable. But even among them the benefits are 15 times larger than their own financial contribution through the tax system. Altogether, households that send their kids to college bear only some 4 percent of the total costs themselves.[14]

Taxing university graduates later in life does not make up for this preferential treatment. Grüske summarizes:

> In none of the scenarios analyzed do the beneficiaries of publicly financed tertiary education even come close to paying back the value of the services received! . . . The gap is financed by . . . non-college graduates who pay up to 90 percent of the entire cost for educating university students.[15]

Of course, it could be argued that blue-collar workers also benefit from the existence of a broad class of well-trained university graduates. For that reason, making them share part of the cost burden might be justifiable. But 90 percent?

That share is much smaller in the United States. America's system of tertiary education, it can therefore be argued, produces more economic justice, not only because it apparently provides more equal opportunities but also because it involves less redistribution from the bottom to the top.

19. The American Dream Lives

"I left England when I was four because I found out I could never be King," Bob Hope loved to say. He never made head of state in his new home country, either, nor could he have, for that matter. But the point remains.

The myth Hope was referring to is at least as old as the United States itself: in America anyone can make it to the top. And that American Dream lives on. Gallup Organization polls regularly show that more than 30 percent of Americans are convinced that one day they, too, will strike it rich.[1] In early 2003, 51 percent of 18- to 29-year-olds thought that the future promised them riches. And even among Americans with household incomes of less than $30,000, 21 percent held that belief.[2]

Social mobility gives people the opportunity to better their lot and to improve their position within society. It is a deciding factor in a society's ability to provide economic justice: a shortage of mobility would reflect a lack of equal opportunities. A high degree of social mobility, on the other hand, can make greater imbalances of income and the distribution of wealth more bearable: if everything is in flux, lifetime incomes will be far more evenly distributed than annual incomes.

The problem is that social mobility is difficult to define and even more difficult to measure. What type of society has the greater social mobility? The society with high fluctuation between social classes? One in which switching between professions is easy? Or maybe a society that has high mobility of income? The latter presumably comes with movement between social classes and movement among professions, but that isn't necessarily so all the time and everywhere.

Income mobility is certainly the easiest form of mobility to measure, though even that is difficult. Absolute and relative mobility, for example, need to be looked at separately. Absolute income mobility exists when income levels of individuals change in absolute terms. Relative income mobility, on the other hand, means that one's

189

Figure 19.1
INCOME MOBILITY OF IMMIGRANTS IN THE UNITED STATES
(MEDIAN HOUSEHOLD INCOME BY NATIVITY, LENGTH OF RESIDENCE IN THE UNITED STATES, AND CITIZENSHIP STATUS OF THE HOUSEHOLDER, 2001, IN DOLLARS)

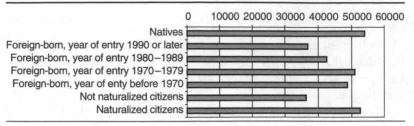

SOURCE: U.S. Census Bureau (www.census.gov).

income level in relation to others' changes.[3] One might assume absolute mobility to be the more crucial one. That would, after all, indicate that the road to prosperity is open to everyone who tries. But relative income mobility, too, is important—not least because the happiness of many people depends not on their standard of living alone but also on how it compares with that of the Joneses: their neighbors, friends, and colleagues.

It's the Feeling That Matters

Income mobility in the United States is undoubtedly significant. To see why, it is helpful to look at the case of immigrants, a group that typically starts at the bottom of the income ladder. The median household income of immigrants who came to the United States after 1989 was 32 percent below the average of native households in 2001 (Figure 19.1). For immigrants who entered the United States in the 1980s, the gap was notably smaller at 21 percent. For immigrants who settled even earlier, in the 1970s, the distance from the average was only 6 percent. And naturalized citizens were a mere 2 percent behind.

However, it's never been proven that the stereotype of countless dishwashers becoming millionaires in America is more than a myth. Indisputable empirical proof that America enjoys an *extraordinary* range of social mobility simply can't be found. It can't even be proven that social mobility is any greater in the United States than in Germany or France. The results of the empirical studies that exist are inconclusive.[4]

That may be partly a problem of measurability. As already mentioned, analyzing income distribution can be tricky. And it's all the more difficult to undertake analyses that track individual incomes both over time and across borders.[5]

Scientists who study mobility empirically usually focus on objective analyses of the sort that can be derived from income statistics. Perceived mobility, however, is easier to measure, and it is not as insignificant as it may seem at first glance. Indeed, it is very important, as much for the regular guy as for politicians who seek reelection. After all, individual well-being depends on how people assess their prospects. Or, in the words of the German pollster Klaus-Peter Schöppner: "Nothing more determines people's attitude to life than whether policies and the economy succeed in creating optimism for the future—regardless of the actual economic situation."[6]

Obviously, such optimism is far more widespread in America than it is in Europe. In 1991, 59 percent of Germans surveyed said that personal success in life is determined by forces that are outside their own control. In the spring of 2003, that sentiment was voiced by 68 percent. Clear majorities agreed with this statement in France and Italy as well. In the United States, by contrast, the sense of empowerment is much stronger (Figure 19.2).

Such drastic differences in attitudes may help to explain why the welfare state is more prevalent in Europe. But the reality is more complicated than that, as a study by Alberto Alesina, Rafael Di Tella, and Robert MacCulloch has pointed out.[7] Those three economists analyzed opinion surveys from the United States and the European Union. Americans and Europeans were both assigned to categories according to income. For convenience's sake, people with above-average income were labeled "rich," those with less were labeled "poor." On the basis of that categorization, Alesina and his colleagues studied what effects inequality has on personal well-being. They controlled for the influence that education, marital status, age, or gender might have. You might assume that the rich on both sides of the Atlantic would be against top-to-bottom redistribution, since it would be at their expense, while the poor would welcome such redistribution.

But the results the three researchers came up with show something rather different:

Figure 19.2
SENSE OF PERSONAL EMPOWERMENT IN THE UNITED STATES,
FRANCE, ITALY, AND GERMANY
(IS SUCCESS DETERMINED BY FORCES OUTSIDE OUR CONTROL?
ANSWERS IN PERCENT)

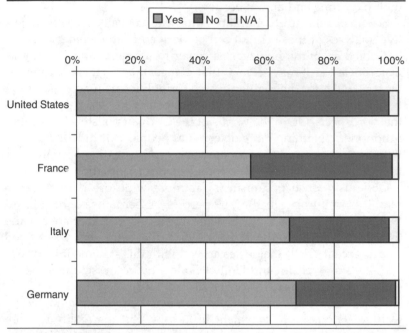

SOURCE: Pew Research Center for the People and the Press (2003), p. 108.

- "Poor" Europeans, regardless of political ideology, do show a strong adverse attitude toward unevenly distributed incomes. "Rich" Europeans, however, are indifferent to inequality.
- In the United States, on the other hand, it's the "poor" who, regardless of their political leaning, don't care so much about inequality. It's the "rich" who are offended by such disparity.

Those results shake the easy prejudice that Americans in general show little appetite for distributive justice. The patterns of attitudes are better explained by differences between Americans and Europeans in perceived mobility.

The following interpretation seems plausible: In the United States the average rich person approves of redistribution because she perceives her attained status as precarious and therefore wants a social safety net to be provided just in case she needs it. In Europe it's the average poor person who favors redistribution because he doesn't believe he has the opportunity to move up.

That pattern could explain why redistribution in America is much more efficiently directed toward the needy than it is in Europe (see Chapter 15). To simplify matters a bit: The well-to-do in the United States want to be insured against the consequences of, say, a job loss. Therefore, they have an interest in welfare measures that actually help those in need. Not so in continental Europe: When the rich feel secure in their status, they have no interest in a top-to-bottom redistribution. Instead they will see to it that money taken by the state from their left pocket is channeled right back into their right pocket.

Of course, it is a social problem when the better-off live in fear of losing their prosperity, as seems to be the case in the United States. However, it is surely debatable whether the European pattern is more desirable. Or is it clearly preferable to live in a society in which the rich are not afraid for their status but the worse-off view their fate as sealed?

20. Better Securely Unemployed Than Insecurely Employed?

American Conditions: Employers can sack employees from one day to the next.

American Conditions: A person who loses her job is eligible for unemployment benefits for six to nine months. If she's single and doesn't have kids, she can receive only noncash transfers such as food stamps thereafter—but only for a while.

American Conditions: Lose your job, lose your health insurance. Only those who are pregnant, handicapped, or have underage children can take refuge under Medicaid.

Even those who are spared unemployment can be hit hard. In cyclical downturns, voluntary benefits are often among the first things that fall victim to corporate cost cutting. And when the stock market crashes, many older employees are forced to work longer than they had planned. When, for instance, the boom of the 1990s ended, it was telling that the labor force participation of younger Americans declined while that of older workers grew. At the end of 2000, 46 percent of 60- to 64-year-olds in the United States were employed; at the end of 2003, the share was just shy of 50 percent.[1]

The vast majority of Americans recovers quickly from such setbacks. Almost half the households that slip below the poverty line are back above it within four months (see Chapter 9). And half of those who lose their health insurance don't stay uninsured for more than five months.[2]

Still, America's economic model doubtlessly exposes millions of citizens to social hardships—social hardships from which the large continental European countries try to shield their citizens. In Germany, for instance, everyone is entitled to unconditional support from the government: According to German law, people have the right to receive the means necessary to afford, among other things, food, clothing, housing, household appliances, and "personal needs" including "participation in cultural life." That assistance, called *Sozialhilfe*, is supposed to help people who can't help themselves but is paid even to those who have deliberately caused their own neediness.

Does that kind of safety net really make people better off? Does it really mean that people feel more secure?

The American Jungle

Gerhard Schröder likes to talk about employment protection legislation when he defends his country's economic model. The German chancellor has said:

> Our land has not gotten to where it is through the laws of the jungle, through unscrupulous hiring and firing, but through self-confident workers, whose motivation is not fear but the will to achieve something together with hard-working entrepreneurs.[3]

"Laws of the jungle," certainly, is a reference to U.S.-style cowboy capitalism. On another occasion, Schröder talked about

> precisely that type of insecurity for the employed known as "American conditions," namely "hire and fire," hiring and kicking out again, without security for the employees. That's not a model after which I strive; I leave that to others. We create a clean balance between flexibility for companies and security and predictability for the households of the employed. They're human beings, and they can't simply be turned into a vast manipulable mass.[4]

That "clean balance" manifests itself in Germany (and in France and Italy) in employment protection legislation that's among the strictest in OECD countries (Figure 20.1). The United States has, in accordance with its reputation, the laxest employment protections.

Does that mean that there's more firing in the United States? One would assume so. A direct comparison, however, isn't possible, because comparable statistics simply don't exist.[5] What is certain, though, is that firing is not quite as common in the United States as the chancellor's "unscrupulous hiring and firing" suggests. In January 2002, 31 percent of employed Americans had been with the same company for 10 or more years. Half of the employees between the ages of 45 and 54 had been with their employers for at least 7.6 years, and half of the 55- to 64-year-olds had a tenure of 9.9 years

Figure 20.1
Strictness of Employment Protection Legislation
(weighted average of indicators for regular contracts,
temporary contracts, and collective dismissals; scores
from 0 to 6, with higher values representing stricter
regulation; late 1990s)

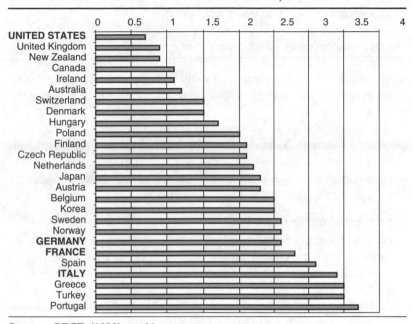

Source: OECD (1999), p. 66.

or more. Although average tenure for those age groups had fallen by about two years since the early 1980s,[6] those numbers hardly lend credence to the idea that average Americans have to live in daily fear of being laid off.

However, even though the average unemployment rate in the 1990s was lower than in the 1980s, the share of people laid off was roughly the same in both decades. That phenomenon is compatible with the assumption that technological progress has sped up structural change (see Chapters 3, 4, and 15).

What's more important for the discussion here, however, is that the share of the employed between the ages of 20 and 64 who lost jobs within a given three-year period is at a longtime average of

10.4 percent. That number certainly hides the fact that certain groups—low-skilled workers, for example—are hit harder than the average person, and that is not to be taken lightly: Anyone who is unemployed in the United States is under enormous pressure to find a new job soon. Also, depending on the state of the economy, the average unemployed person has to take cuts in earnings as great as 12 percent in order to get a new job.[7]

But those setbacks will be the exception in the working life of an average employee. A 10.4 percent average likelihood of losing a job within three years means that the chance of losing a job in two consecutive three-year periods is only 1.1 percent. The probability of losing jobs in three consecutive three-year periods is accordingly a mere .1 percent.

The question then is whether the 10 percent risk of losing a job once in three years is really so unbearable that no one should be burdened with it. Perhaps. Still, the risk is certainly not so high that it should preclude one from looking beyond the disadvantages of "the laws of the jungle" to their advantages.

Doing Good or Meaning Well

From the perspective of employers, employment protection legislation increases the cost of laying off workers. In that sense, it can be viewed as a tax on adjustments to the size and structure of a company's workforce.[8]

Such a tax can be presumed to curb the number of layoffs. Correspondingly, however, companies will also be more hesitant to hire new employees. They'll hang back from increasing their workforce in response to increased demand because they usually can't tell if the increase is going to last; if it isn't, the costs of hiring might well turn out to be higher than the benefits. That's especially clear in the case of start-ups, which naturally have a hard time foreseeing their economic success. Between 1992 and 1997, American start-ups that survived the first years in business expanded their staff by an average of 161 percent within two years. In Germany that increase was only 24 percent, and in France it was a meager 13 percent.[9]

Holding back from hiring means that anyone who, in spite of strict employment legislation, loses a job will have a harder time finding a new one. Economists speak in such cases of an "insider-outsider problem." The employed (insiders) are protected at the expense of the unemployed (outsiders).[10]

In the end, a society must gauge whose interests are more important. At an unemployment rate of 2 or 4 percent, a decision in favor of the insiders might be easy to justify. But can that still be the case when the unemployment rate is at 10 or 12 percent? Is it conscionable when a considerable share of those 10 or 12 percent are long-term unemployed and run the risk of being permanently excluded from a life of gainful employment?

It is certainly possible, however, that rigorous employment protections merely lengthen the average duration of periods of unemployment without any further negative side effects—that is, without increasing overall unemployment. On balance, job protection and job creation would even out, since fewer people would be fired and fewer would be hired. What cannot be determined theoretically is therefore the effect on the *level* of employment. That question can only be answered empirically.[11]

The results of empirical investigation, however, are clear. Employment protection legislation, as currently enforced in France, Germany, and Italy, contributes not only to workers having to look longer for new jobs but also to more people being unemployed. According to calculations by the IMF cited earlier, adoption of America's "laws of the jungle" would lower unemployment rates in Europe by 1.65 percentage points (see Figure 4.3). In Germany, that would roughly translate into employment for some 700,000 people who are currently out of work.[12]

Again, it could be argued that solving the conflict of interest between insiders and outsiders in favor of insiders is justified. Banning 700,000 people from work might be an acceptable price for employment protection that benefits the more than 38 million employees in Germany.

Quite another question is whether German employment protection actually offers those 38 million workers what it is supposed to: a life free from fear of tumbling down the economic ladder. Surveys raise doubts. It turns out, as it so often does, that good intentions don't necessarily yield good results. Sometimes they yield just the opposite.

Better Employment Protection through Full Employment

At the end of 2003, 38 percent of surveyed Americans said that they might face a prolonged search for a new job if they were to

Figure 20.2
EASINESS OF JOB SEARCHES IN THE UNITED STATES, GERMANY, FRANCE, AND ITALY
(HOW EASY WOULD IT BE TO FIND A NEW JOB?
ANSWERS IN PERCENT)

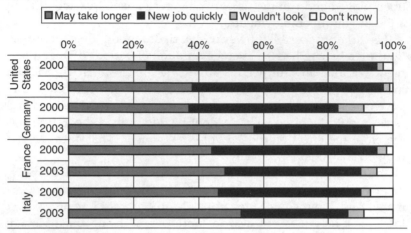

SOURCE: Gallup International (www.gallup-international.com).

become unemployed. In France (48 percent), Italy (53 percent), and Germany (57 percent), that share was notably higher (Figure 20.2).

Those discrepancies are to be expected. But what's surprising is the share of Europeans who, despite their better protection, think that their jobs are in peril. At the end of 2003, 32 percent felt that way in Germany; only 19 percent did in America (Figure 20.3).

Of course, survey results are only snapshots that might be strongly influenced by the current, cyclical state of the economies. But as Figures 20.2 and 20.3 also show, the same transatlantic differences were found at the end of 2000 (and in 2001 and 2002 as well.)[13]

It therefore seems plausible that it's not so much employment protection legislation that creates the feeling of economic security as it is a high level of employment. In the end, a tight labor market will certainly not keep companies from restructuring their labor force in order to ensure that they remain competitive. But employers who are aware that supply on the labor market is scarce will think twice before they engage in "unscrupulous hiring and firing."

Figure 20.3
JOB SECURITY IN THE UNITED STATES, GERMANY,
FRANCE, AND ITALY
(IS YOUR JOB SAFE? ANSWERS IN PERCENT)

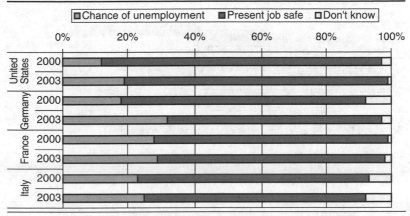

SOURCE: Gallup International (www.gallup-international.com).

Happy Days—In America

Life is more than just work, and economic security is more than just a secure job. It's therefore only natural at this point to look at numbers that show how secure people generally feel in America and Europe. Unfortunately, no surveys suitable for comparison seem to be available.

But there are surveys in which participants on both sides of the Atlantic were asked to assess their own lives. If, as the German chancellor suggests, Americans are driven by fear while the continental European model provides "security and predictability," that should be reflected in the results of those surveys. After all, it can be reasonably expected that fear—fear for one's job, fear for one's social status, fear of poverty—considerably lessens one's sense of well-being.

Forty-nine percent of Americans said in April 2003 that their personal situation was better than it had been five years earlier (Figure 20.4). That might not be a strikingly high percentage, but look at what happened during those five years: a prolonged stock market downturn, a recession followed by an initially slow recovery, and, certainly, 9/11. In any case, the share of people who said their

201

Figure 20.4
LIFE SATISFACTION AND OPTIMISM IN THE UNITED STATES, ITALY, FRANCE, AND GERMANY
(POLL RESULTS OF APRIL 2003 (USA) AND SPRING 2002 (EUROPE))

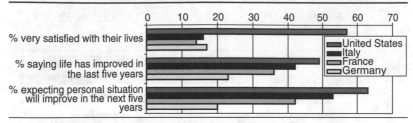

SOURCE: Harris Interactive (www.harrisinteractive.com).

Figure 20.5
LIFE DISSATISFACTION AND PESSIMISM IN THE UNITED STATES, ITALY, FRANCE, AND GERMANY
(POLL RESULTS OF APRIL 2003 (USA) AND SPRING 2002 (EUROPE))

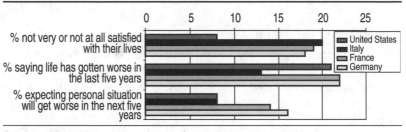

SOURCE: Harris Interactive (www.harrisinteractive.com)

situation had improved was a lot higher in America than in Italy and France—and more than twice as high as in Germany.

On the other hand, while the share of people who thought their situation had gotten worse over the last five years was about the same in the United States, France, and Germany, it was significantly smaller in Italy (Figure 20.5). Thus, in that respect, the United States evidently has nothing on the European nations. But wouldn't one expect the number to be much higher in America—the alleged home of the laws of the jungle—than in Europe?

It is true, as argued in Chapter 19, that many better-off Americans worry about their socioeconomic status. But just how great those worries are is questionable. If Americans live in great fear, it should leave them downtrodden. Figures 20.4 and 20.5, however, also show that most Americans are "very satisfied" with their lives and that not even 1 in 12 is "not very" or "not at all" satisfied. In France, Germany, and Italy, the share of satisfied people is much smaller and the share of the dissatisfied is much larger.

Three times as many Americans as Germans expect that their personal situation will get better in the next five years. Only 8 percent of Americans believe that their lot will worsen, as opposed to 14 percent of the French and 16 percent of Germans. Now who's feeling insecure?

A whole litany of objections could be raised against that line of reasoning. It might be criticized on the grounds that subjective security doesn't matter; objective security is what matters. That, however, is simply untrue. Surely the well-being of persons depends, if only in part, on their own perceptions.

A case could also be made that the survey results presented in Figures 20.4 and 20.5 are only snapshots and were made a year apart (April 2003 in the United States, spring of 2002 in the European Union). The differences are so large, though, that it seems unlikely that they would simply disappear if the surveys were repeated.

In addition, it might be argued that Americans are generally more optimistic than Europeans, so perhaps Americans would show more confidence even under economic conditions identical to those in Europe. That claim has something to it. Everything will be well, promised Franklin D. Roosevelt, when he toured the country during his election campaign at the height of the depression in 1932. FDR had his staff play over and over, "Happy days are here again, the skies above are clear again." You can't find any accounts in the history books of anyone singing about happier days and blue skies before the German elections in 1932, just before voters swept Hitler to power.

It's also conceivable that Americans don't like to show their pessimism. Demonstrative optimism as an expression of collective perseverance after 9/11, too, could be a reason. But again, the discrepancies are so large that it's doubtful that such factors alone can explain them.

It therefore seems likely that there's another reason for the differences. That reason could simply be the consciousness of Americans that they live in a prosperous country. Could it be that the relatively higher risks of losing a job or health insurance become acceptable when it's at the same time more likely that those losses will be overcome within a matter of a few months? Could it be that continually high economic growth and job creation help to make people feel more secure than do all those welfare state handouts and regulations?

Admittedly, it can't be proven here that the answer to these questions is yes. But that the answer is indeed yes seems plausible, to say the least.

Conclusion

> We are suffering just now from a bad attack of economic pessimism. It is common to hear people say that the epoch of enormous economic progress which characterized the nineteenth century is over. . . . I believe that this is a widely mistaken interpretation of what is happening to us. We are suffering, not from the rheumatics of old age, but from the growing-pains of over-rapid changes, from the painfulness of readjustment between one economic period and another.
>
> John Maynard Keynes, 1930[1]

France, Germany, and Italy are prosperous countries. The overwhelming majority of people enjoy a standard of living that would, just a few generations ago, have been considered obscene.

The economic models of those three countries evidently worked well for decades after World War II. That alone makes it foolish to claim that those models are generally, under all imaginable circumstances, inferior to other economic models.

But the French, Germans, and Italians got rich during times in which technological progress was relatively slow and the pressure to adjust quickly was accordingly low. It was a time when global competition was relatively weak and economic policy mistakes had a much smaller observable impact, if only because there were many other governments that made far more basic mistakes—remember communism?

Maybe those times are bound to return—sometime. Currently, however, there's no reason to think so.

Meanwhile, the American model seems to be far better equipped for the "age of Schumpeter," as Herbert Giersch called it, with its drastically increased pressures to adapt. It's hard to see any other convincing conclusion from a European-American comparison of growth and employment over the last 25 years.

Then why not just bid adieu to Euro-style "comfy capitalism"? European politicians tell us that we shouldn't because it creates fewer social problems than U.S.-style "cowboy capitalism" and because it offers more economic justice and security. At a closer look, however, the picture of the United States as an anti-social country proves to be a bundle of prejudices and stereotypes, which are largely divorced from reality. Quite a number of them are myths that have taken on lives of their own.

Of course, gross injustices and major social problems do exist in the United States. The lack of health insurance for millions is one. The continuing poverty of single mothers and their kids and the dysfunctional public school system and the ridiculously high salaries of many management executives are others. But these phenomena are not, for the most part at least, the price Americans pay for freewheeling, dynamic cowboy capitalism. They could all be solved or ameliorated without the United States' moving more than an iota toward European comfy capitalism.

* * *

The propensity for larger discrepancies of income and wealth is, however, an integral element of the American model. That is a price Americans currently are paying for their system, but it is at the same time a crucial precondition for the presence of the entrepreneurs and highly qualified employees necessary for quick and smooth adjustment to rapid technological progress and global competition.

Are such American conditions therefore more unjust than continental European ones? If economic justice means that people are rewarded according to their efforts, then clearly the American model delivers superior results. When in France, Germany, and Italy a (growing) minority is de facto paid by the government for keeping away from the labor market, that can't be reconciled with such an ideal of justice. When, at the same time, a (shrinking) majority faces marginal tax burdens somewhat greater than 60 percent, that, too, can hardly be considered fair.

Certainly, economic justice is more than proportionality of reward to effort. Another important element is equal opportunity. There again, the United States also arguably gets closer to the ideal than the three large continental European countries. It's in France, Germany, and Italy, not in America, that millions of people are locked out of the labor market for long periods of time. France, Germany, and Italy, not America, are more and more turning into two-class societies consisting of those who are employed and those who are not.

Educational opportunities may not be distributed fairly in the United States, but they're distributed a lot more fairly than in Germany, especially. Germany, not the United States, is the country where a student's educational success depends more on the socioeconomic status of her parents. Germany, not the United States, is the country where fewer children of low-income parents go to college. And all that is true despite the fact that Germany's rejection of college tuitions constitutes a blatant violation of what is called "social justice" in German political debate.

To be sure, there is less "social justice" in America than elsewhere if that term means that every citizen is unconditionally entitled to a certain minimum income. However, the American model does help people in need—but not without time limits nor without any regard to the individual's willingness to help himself. Support for households that can't make ends meet with their earned income alone does exist, but it's coupled to the individual's own efforts via the Earned Income Tax Credit.

And, yes, France, Germany, and Italy create more "social justice" if the sheer amount of redistribution is considered. But when one considers how much money is just moved back and forth rather than actually from the top to the bottom of the income ladder, the picture looks quite different again. It's Germany and Italy, not America, where the better-off pay a smaller share of the tax revenue. It's in Germany and Italy, not America, where a disproportionately large share of cash transfers goes to the rich.

* * *

In addition to the relatively pronounced unequal distribution of income, discomfort is another symptom of cowboy capitalism. The American model demands mobility from the individual—not only in the geographical sense of the word.

But just as inequality is not synonymous with injustice, discomfort is not the same as insecurity. Take the labor market as an example. If economic security means that everyone has a right to work a lifetime in the profession she once learned or never has to leave a living place or a job once attained, yes, then continental Europe does better.

Or, more precisely, continental Europe *used* to provide more security. In the France, Germany, and Italy of *today*, at best you find the illusion of such security. And that's only at the price of guaranteeing a growing minority a completely different kind of security; namely, the security of being excluded from gainful employment for long periods of time or even indefinitely.

American conditions on continental European labor markets, on the other hand, would mean that the average employee would have an annual risk of being fired of about 4 percent. But they would also mean that the jobless would have a 65 percent chance of finding a new employer within three months—instead of a chance of 26 percent (France), 18 percent (Germany), or even only 12 percent (Italy).[2]

Such conditions may not necessarily create a greater feeling of security, even though the comparison of surveys in Chapter 20 indicates that they do precisely that. But what would surely be achieved is a more even distribution of economic risks. More people would be hit, but any particular person would be hit less hard. In that sense, American conditions are exactly the opposite of how they are depicted in Europe. By the criteria of their staunchest critics, American conditions, in that sense, are more just than those in Europe.

* * *

American conditions? In Europe? Of course not. No one would seriously suggest copying one economic model, no matter which, in another country.

But what speaks against Americanizing the continental European economies by a good margin? Why not pursue reforms that would allow the inhabitants of countries such as France, Germany, and Italy to reap the benefits of the American model? The real problems that come along with American capitalism could for the most part be avoided, especially because, after all, they have nothing or little to do with cowboy capitalism itself.

And European economic systems need not be as "American" as the American system itself. The success of the American model doesn't stand and fall with the fact that only some Americans enjoy five or six weeks of vacation annually. Nor do all employee protections have to be chucked in order to provide firms and employees with the flexibility they so clearly need in these Schumpeterian times.

Finally, after 20 years of mini-reforms in continental Europe, it can't be expected that European countries run the danger of going too far all of a sudden, anyway. The risk is, if anything, not too much Americanization but too little.

Thus, it's not cowboy capitalism that Europeans ought to fear but the fear of it.

Notes

Introduction

1. OECD (2003) and author's calculations.
2. Statement, April 24, 2002, quoted from www.spd.de.
3. Speech, June 5, 2002, quoted from www.csu.de.
4. *Frankfurter Allgemeine Zeitung* (2002).
5. *Tagesspiegel* (2002).
6. IMF (www.imf.org) and author's calculations.
7. *Der Spiegel* (2003); emphasis added.
8. Moore (2001), p. xvi.
9. Michael Moore (www.michaelmoore.com).
10. Piper Verlag. Moore's U.S. publisher, Regan Books, declines to publish sales numbers.

Chapter 1

1. Vedder and Gallaway (1997), pp. 220ff.
2. Maddison (2001), pp. 304, 308; cf. Greenspan (2003), p. 3.
3. Maddison (2001), pp. 289, 306, 322ff.
4. Sachs (2003).
5. Cf. Acemoglu, Johnson, and Robinson (2002); and IMF (2003), pp. 95ff.
6. Gordon (2002), pp. 5, 13ff.

Chapter 2

1. Beck (1997).
2. *Süddeutsche Zeitung* (2003).
3. See Figure 4.5.
4. Börsch-Supan (2000), p. 3.
5. U.S. Patent and Trademark Office (www.uspto.gov). That Duell actually ever made this often-quoted statement is doubtful.
6. The OECD standardized unemployment rates tend to make European countries look better in comparison with the United States than the nonstandardized rates used here. The OECD measurements, however, do not factor in hidden unemployment and consequently depict a distorted version of reality (see below).
7. BLS (www.bls.gov).
8. Sachverständigenrat zur Begutachtung der gesamtwirtschaftlichen Entwicklung (2003), p. 535; and author's calculations.
9. Author's calculations based on the data used for Figure 2.2.
10. U.S. Census Bureau (www.census.gov).
11. OECD (2003a), pp. 320–21; and author's calculations.

12. Institut für Arbeitsmarkt- und Berufsforschung (2004), p. 9; and author's calculations. Employees who are on maternity leave or in government-sponsored early retirement programs are included in the official statistics but subtracted in the overall employment number mentioned here. Calculations are based on actual hours worked on average by full- and part-time employees in 1996 and 2003, respectively.

13. The hours worked time series, published by the OECD, come from different sources. Therefore, they are better suited for comparisons of trends over time than for international comparisons for a given year. Also, it's assumed here that the annual hours actually worked are the same for all working-age persons. Furthermore, when calculating the hours worked per capita, it's assumed that persons over 64 years of age don't work. Since employment beyond the age of 64 can be considered far more common in the United States than in Europe, the transatlantic differences should in reality be even larger than those displayed in Figures 2.5 and 2.6.

Chapter 3

1. Economists differentiate between several types of productivity. In this chapter, only labor productivity is looked at. The terms "labor productivity" and "productivity" are used interchangeably.

2. Statistical Office of the European Communities database and author's calculations.

3. Gordon (2000).

4. Cf. DeLong (2002), pp. 4–5, and the literature cited there.

5. The productivity indicator most frequently used in the United States refers to the nonfarm business sector. In the numbers mentioned in this section, however, agriculture is included. This is to maximize comparability between U.S. and German data. The German productivity index, compiled by the German central bank, the Deutsche Bundesbank, refers to the whole economy and includes the farm sector (as well as the public sector).

6. For this figure five-year moving averages were chosen because annual growth rates often veer off erratically.

7. Cf. Deutsche Bundesbank (2002), p. 50.

8. Ibid.

9. See, for instance, McGuckin and van Ark (2003), p. 19; and OECD (2003c), p. 34.

10. OECD (2004), p. 241; and author's calculations.

11. Deutsche Bundesbank (2002), p. 63; see also Chapter 4.

12. Council of Economic Advisers (1997), p. 171; and Schmidley (2003), p. 5.

13. See, for example, IMF (2002), pp. 18–19; Jorgenson, Ho, and Stiroh (2003); and Triplett and Bosworth (2003).

14. David (1990), pp. 355ff.

15. Ibid., p. 360.

16. Crafts (2002), p. 2.

17. Ibid., pp. 2, 15.

18. Gordon (2003).

19. McKinsey Global Institute (2001).

20. BLS (www.bls.gov) and Gordon (2003).

21. See, for example, IMF (2002), p. 20; and UBS Warburg (2003), p. 3.

22. Information Technology Association of America (www.itaa.org) and *Business Week* (2002).

23. BEA (www.bea.gov).

24. *Wirtschaftswoche* (2000) and Shop.org (www.shop.org).

25. Field (1980). A significant difference between the railroad and IT is that computers and software are written off within a few years and overinvestment is thus of rather little consequence.

26. Cf. *Wall Street Journal* (2002) and *Forbes* (2003).

27. *Wirtschaftswoche* (2001).

28. Ibid.

29. Cf. Malkiel (2003), p. 75; and Lewis (2002).

30. DeLong (2002a), pp. 294–95.

31. King (2002), pp. 7–8.

32. Ibid., p. 14.

33. Ibid., p. 9.

34. See, for example, Summers and DeLong (2002). That point can be made for ICT-producing industries themselves, too. But there are, as in the offline world, exceptions. For instance, there might be cases in which the consumer benefits all the more from a product the more other consumers use it. The result is a trend toward monopolization. Examples that come to mind are Microsoft's Windows and Ebay.

35. Cf. Summers and DeLong (2002).

36. See, for example, Feldstein (2003), p. 3.

37. Jorgenson, Ho, and Stiroh (2003), pp. 41–42.

38. Cf. David (1990), pp. 357–58; Feldstein (2003), p. 4; Greenspan (2002), p. 3; and IMF (2001), pp. 103ff.

39. Cf. Summers and DeLong (2002a).

40. DeLong (2002), pp. 33ff.

Chapter 4

1. Council of Economic Advisers (2004), p. 378.

2. Yergin and Stanislaw (2002), pp. 356ff.

3. Ibid., pp. 362ff. American savings banks were allowed to invest deposits in more risky ventures without any consequent reduction of the federal guarantee of these deposits. This was one of the reasons for the savings & loan crisis in the late 1980s.

4. Alesina, Ardagna, Nicoletti, and Schiantarelli (2003), p. 2, and the literature cited there.

5. *Wall Street Journal* (2001).

6. Agency for Children and Families (www.acf.dhhs.gov). Since implementation in 1997, the number of single mothers with jobs has increased by ten percentage points; the poverty rate of families with single mothers shrank by a third and was at the historical low of 24.7 percent in 2000. Blank (2002), pp. 1115ff.

7. Greenspan (2003), p. 2.

8. National Right to Work Legal Defense Foundation (www.nrtw.org).

9. U.S. Department of Labor (2001), p. 69; BLS (www.bls.gov); and author's calculations.

10. An extensive but not exhaustive list of new labor regulations can be found in Krueger (2000), p. 302; cf. Freeman (2000).

11. Crews (2003), pp. 1–2.

12. Gwartney and Lawson (2003), pp. 13ff.

13. Cf. Bertola, Blau, and Kahn (2001), p. 163; and Sinn (2002), pp. 25–26.

14. OECD.

15. OECD (www.oecd.org); cf. Sinn (2002), p. 18; and Sachverständigenrat zur Begutachtung der gesamtwirtschaftlichen Entwicklung (2002), p. 10.

16. Commission of the European Communities (2002), p. 43.

17. Ibid., p. 2.

18. OECD (www.oecd.org) and author's calculations.

19. Cf. Commission of the European Communities (2002), p. 43.

20. Sinn (2002), pp. 7, 22.

21. Cf., for instance, Deutsches Institut für Wirtschaftsforschung (2004), pp. 26–27.

22. IMF (2002), p. 129. Similar results are attained by studies of Garibaldi and Mauro (1999) for the labor market and by Alesina, Ardagna, Nicoletti, and Schiantarelli (2003) for product markets.

23. OECD (2003b), pp. 28–29; and author's calculations.

24. OECD (2000), p. 96; and author's calculations.

25. Cf. OECD (2000a), p. 47.

26. Cf. Howard (2002), pp. 83ff.; and Cohen, Dickens und Posen (2001), p. 220.

27. Cf. IMF (2003), p. 137.

28. Statistisches Bundesamt (2003), pp. 44, 76; Schachter (2001), p. 2; and author's calculations.

29. Schachter (2001), p. 3; and *Washington Post* (2003).

30. BLS (www.bls.gov) and author's calculations.

31. IMF (2003), p. 136; and Bundesagentur für Arbeit (2004), p. 33.

32. Cf. Krueger and Kumar (2002).

33. Cf. Industrie- und Handelskammer Nord-Westfalen (www.ihk-muenster.de).

34. *Handelsblatt* (1998).

35. Cf. Wasmer (2003), pp. 3ff., 24ff.

36. Ibid.; Krueger and Kumar (2002); and Krueger and Kumar (2004).

37. OECD; cf. Scarpetta, Hemmings, Tressel, and Woo (2002), p. 43.

38. Djankov, La Porta, Lopes-de-Silanes, and Schleifer (2002).

39. An analysis with alternative methods of calculation comes up with different, but comparable numbers. Scarpetta, Hemmings, Tressel, and Woo (2002), p. 40.

40. Ibid., pp. 12–13.

41. *BusinessWeek online* (www.businessweek.com).

42. Global Insight, U.S. Census Bureau (www.census.gov), and author's calculations.

43. Bundesministerium für Bildung und Forschung (2003), p. 110.

44. David (1990).

45. Baily (2003), p. 9.

46. Ibid., p. 7; Feldstein (2003), pp. 5–6; and Home Depot (www.homedepot.com).

47. *Wirtschaftswoche* (2001a), pp. 78ff.; and *Wirtschaftswoche* (2002), pp. 50ff.

48. Feldstein (2003), p. 5; Greenspan (2000), p. 2; and Hubbard (2002), p. 3.

49. Giersch (1999), pp. 19–20; cf. Sachverständigenrat zur Begutachtung der gesamtwirtschaftlichen Entwicklung (2002), pp. 9, 215.

50. Bertola, Blau, and Kahn (2001); cf. Blanchard and Wolfers (2000).

51. Cf. Blinder and Yellen (2001), pp. 94–95; and Roach (1998).

52. Cox and Alm (1999), p. 122; and US60 (www.us60.com); data on the websites of the companies mentioned; and author's calculations. Due to mergers and takeovers, some of those companies now have different names.

53. Deutsches Aktieninstitut and author's calculations.

Chapter 5

1. NBER (www.nber.org); and Roach (2003), p. 1. Numbers are not adjusted for purchasing power parities.
2. Cf. Business Cycle Dating Committee (2003), pp. 2ff.
3. Ibid.; cf. IMF (2002a), p. 5.
4. BEA (www.bea.gov).
5. Ibid. and author's calculations.
6. BEA (www.bea.gov); preliminary data published in March 2004.
7. Institute of International Finance (www.iif.com).
8. Freund (2000), p. 8; BEA (www.bea.gov); and author's calculations.
9. Expenses for military research and development can, of course, have spillover effects. The most prominent example of Pentagon money having had a positive effect on productivity is surely the Internet, which the U.S. military originally developed as a means of internal communication.
10. Council of Economic Advisers (2004), p. 378.
11. Laubach (2003).
12. BEA (www.bea.gov); Council of Economic Advisers (2004), p. 378; and author's calculations.
13. Council of Economic Advisers (2004), p. 377; and author's calculations.
14. Jackson (2003), p. 14.
15. Author's calculation based on data used for Figure 2.2.

Chapter 6

1. Cf. Gordon (2002), p. 11.
2. Schneider (2003), p. 7.
3. BJS (www.ojp.usdoj.gov/bjs) and International Centre for Prison Studies (www.kcl.ac.uk/depsta/rel/icps).
4. BJS (www.ojp.usdoj.gov/bjs) and author's calculations.
5. Sanchez, Lang, and Dhavale (2003), pp. 8–9.
6. Speech in the Bundestag, October 29, 2002, quoted from www.bundesregierung.de.
7. Blanchflower and Oswald (2004), for instance, prove the following: Statistically, surveyed divorced Americans are only as happy as their married countrymen when they, under otherwise identical circumstances, earn over $100,000 more per year.
8. Gordon (2002), p. 12.
9. Ibid., (2002), p. 10.
10. OECD (2004), p. 241.
11. World Bank (2003), pp. 15–16, 89–90, 123–24. All data are for 2001.
12. Speech in the Bundestag.

Chapter 7

1. U.S. Chamber of Commerce (2004).
2. Aizcorbe, Kennickell, and Moore (2003), p. 16; and Deutsches Aktieninstitut (www.dai.de).
3. U.S. Census Bureau (2003), p. 2.
4. It is of importance here that the median and not the mean is being considered. An average can rise solely by the rich getting richer while all other incomes stagnate. With a median that is, by definition, not possible. The median, after all, is the point that divides the top from the bottom 50 percent of income earners.

5. U.S. Census Bureau (www.census.gov); U.S. Census Bureau (2002), p. 8; U.S. Census Bureau (2003) , p. 15; and author's calculations.

6. Aizcorbe, Kennckell, and Moore (2003), p. 19.

7. Hourly wages are used here in order to be able to include most recent developments. That means that taxes paid are ignored; thus, the calculations might be considered misleading. However, since, as argued above, the tax burden declined after 1980, the increase of purchasing power as presented in Table 7.2 is, if anything, underestimated.

Chapter 8

1. Federal Reserve Board (www.federalreserve.gov); and Dynan, Johnson, and Pence (2003), p. 243.

2. *Der Spiegel* (2003); italics added.

3. Reuters, March 2003.

4. BEA (www.bea.gov) and author's calculations.

5. Peach and Steindel (2000), p. 1.

6. Ibid., p. 2.

7. Federal Reserve Board (www.federalreserve.gov).

8. Cf. Aizcorbe, Kennickell, and Murphy (2003), p. 21; Peach and Steindel (2000), p. 4; and UBS Warburg (2002), p. 6.

9. Deutsche Bundesbank (2002a), p. 31, points out that in Germany, unlike the United States, the companies of self-employed persons are included in household debt statistics. That means that indebtedness in Germany is shown as too high in comparison with America. But the same, of course, is true for the assessment of assets. For a discussion of further delineation difficulties, see Babeau and Sbano (2003), pp. 33ff.

10. Cf. DeKaser (2003), p. 1; Greenspan (2004); and Peach and Steindel (2000), p. 4.

11. Federal Reserve Board (www.federalreserve.gov). The reliability of these numbers and suggested trends is questionable. The "Survey of Consumer Finances" that is conducted every three years by the Federal Reserve points to a trend in the opposite direction. According to the most recent issue, debt service in 2001 was the lowest it had been since 1989. Aizcorbe, Kennickell, and Moore (2003), p. 1.

12. BEA (www.bea.gov) and author's calculations.

13. BEA (www.bea.gov) and author's calculations.

14. BankcruptcyData.Com (www.bankcruptcydata.com).

15. American Banker's Association (www.aba.com); Mortgage Bankers' Association (www.mbaa.org); and UBS Warburg (2002), p. 6.

16. DeKaser (2003), p. 1; and Federal Reserve Board (www.federalreserve.gov).

17. Natcher (2002), p. 1.

18. Hatzius (2003), p. 6.

19. Greenspan (2004).

20. BEA (www.bea.gov) and author's calculations.

Chapter 9

1. United Nations Development Programme (2003), p. 248. The numbers refer to the years 1990 to 2000.

2. Maddison (2001), p. 276; and author's calculations.

216

3. The standard calculations refer to *mean* incomes *per capita*. As mentioned in Chapter 6, the U.S. average is about 42 percent above the German average. The difference of the respective *medians* is presumably smaller due to the more pronounced income inequality in the United States (see Chapter 15).

4. Maddison (2001), p. 276; and author's calculations.

5. U.S. Census Bureau (2003), p. 22.

6. Cf. Haveman (2000), pp. 272ff.

7. Jargowsky (2003), p. 4. High-poverty neighborhoods are defined here as communities where the poverty rate is 40 percent or higher.

8. U.S. Census Bureau (2003a), pp. 22ff.; and author's calculations. Cf. Haveman (2000), p. 249.

9. Naifeh (1998).

10. For comparison, the official poverty rate was at 15.4 and 15.7 percent in 1993 and 1994, respectively. The discrepancy occurs because the official poverty rate is calculated on the basis of annual incomes. In the study under discussion, however, monthly incomes were being considered. Ibid., p. 1.

11. Ibid., pp. 2ff.

12. BLS (2004), Table 1; and author's calculations.

13. Eberstadt (2002).

14. Cox and Alm (1999), p. 15.

15. U.S. Census Bureau (www.census.gov).

16. Haveman (2000), pp. 249, 262ff., 267.

17. Ibid., p. 268; and author's calculations. Calculated in 1996 dollars, the expenditures rose from $196 million in 1978 to $373 million in 1996.

18. Friedman (1982), p. 192.

19. Cf. Sinn (2002), pp. 28ff.

20. Council of Economic Advisers (2003), p. 120.

21. U.S. Census Bureau (www.census.gov) and author's calculations.

22. Bertrand and Mullainathan (2003).

23. Haveman (2000), p. 252; and U.S. Census Bureau (2003a), p. 33.

24. U.S. Census Bureau (www.census.gov); and U.S. Census Bureau (2003), p. 19.

25. Quoted from U.S. Department of Labor (www.dol.gov).

26. Caplow, Hicks, and Wattenberg (2001), p. 83; McKinnon (2003), p. 3; and U.S. Census Bureau (www.census.gov).

27. Ibid.

28. Naifch (1998), p. 6.

29. One of the reasons is statistical in nature: When calculating the official poverty line significant economies of scale are assumed. That means that it is taken as given that a four-person household needs far less money than two two-person households. The result is that a four-person household with an annual income of $20,000 is not considered poor. If this household is split, say by divorce, into two two-person households, at least one of those households will invariably fall below the poverty line. If the annual income is roughly divided in equal parts, both households slip into official poverty. Cf. Haveman (2000), p. 249; and U.S. Census Bureau (www.census.gov).

30. Administration for Children and Families (www.acf.dhhs.gov).

31. Committee on Ways and Means (2000), p. 465; and Sorensen and Oliver (2002).

32. Gilder (1993), pp. 12, 82.

33. Centers for Disease Prevention and Control (www.cdc.gov).

Chapter 10

1. *Wirtschaftwoche* (1997).
2. BLS (2003a), Tables 1 and 10; *Wall Street Journal* (2001); and author's calculations.
3. OECD (2003d), p. 151
4. Garibaldi and Mauro (1999), p. 12.
5. Cf. for instance Council of Economic Advisers (1997), pp. 140ff. An overview of the empirical literature can be found in Freeman (2000).
6. Ilg and Haugen (2000), p. 22.
7. Figure 10.1 is constructed after Figures 1 and 2 in Ilg and Haugen (2000), pp. 24–25. Randy Ilg was so kind as to provide an updated version of the data. Further updates are not forthcoming because of the introduction of a new statistical classification system in 2003. Comparable data going further back are not available either.
8. U.S. Department of Commerce (2002), pp. 42–43; U.S. Department of Commerce (2003), pp. 21ff; and author's calculations.
9. Wright and Dwyer (2003), p. 301.
10. OECD (2000), p. 96; and author's calculations. Data for Germany are not available.
11. Mosisa (2003), p. 13.
12. With 1,900 work hours a year at the current minimum wage, a gross income of $9,785 is attained. The poverty level for a single adult under 65 years was $9,359 in 2002. U.S. Census Bureau (2003a), p. 4; and author's calculations.
13. U.S. Bureau of Labor Statistics (2003b), Table 1.
14. That's the reason why an increase of the minimum wage, even if it were not to reduce the number of available jobs, would be an inefficient tool for fighting poverty: rather than helping the truly needy, it would increase incomes of households across the board. Wu, Perloff, and Golan (2002), p. 11.

Chapter 11

1. Cf. Putnam (2002), pp. 194ff.
2. Cf. Wright and Dwyer (2003), p. 310.
3. Cf. Freeman (2000).
4. Commission of the European Communities (2002a), p. 9. Note that the "employment ratio" covers only people who are actually employed; the "labor force participation rate" displayed in Figure 11.2 also includes people who are registered as unemployed.
5. Juhn and Murphy (1997), p. 74.
6. U.S. Census Bureau (2002), p. 373; and Statistisches Bundesamt (2003a), Table 15. Data for Germany are for April 2002; those for the United States are for 2001. Note that the number for the United States also includes women who are unemployed. On the other hand, only married women are included in the American data; married women do have lower labor force participation than single, divorced, or widowed women (who are included in the German data).
7. U.S. Bureau of Labor Statistics (www.bls.gov).
8. Company disclosures. In the data for Germany, Dresdner Bank and Allianz Dresdner Asset Management, two major subdivisions, are not included.
9. Catalyst (www.catalystwomen.org).
10. *Fortune* (2003).
11. U.S. Department of Education (2003), p. 103.

12. U.S. Census Bureau (2002), p. 381.

13. U.S. Bureau of Labor Statistics (2003b), p. 35. All numbers are medians. All data on income per hour refer solely to wage and salary workers paid hourly rates.

14. The Roper Center for Public Opinion Research (www.ropercenter.uconn.edu).

15. Juhn and Murphy (1997), pp. 74ff.

16. Ibid., p. 75.

Chapter 12

1. *Einblick* (2002).

2. BLS.

3. The picture is different when women and men are looked at separately. In 1970 multiple jobs were three times more common for men than for women. Today, women have a slight edge on men when it comes to working at more than one job. It seems plausible to attribute that to the 1996 welfare reform. However, the big increase in multiple job holding among women occurred during the 1970s and 1980s. And despite welfare reform, it has been trending downward since the mid-1990s. Cf. Stinson (1997), p. 4.

4. Institut für Arbeitsmarkt- und Berufsforschung (2004), p. 9.

5. Sinn (2002), p. 18.

6. Ibid. and author's calculations.

7. Calculated on the basis of May 2001 employment data.

8. Analyses from 1989 and 1997 hint at economic need having been a more important issue then. See Martel (2000) and Stinson (1990). It is, however, difficult to compare the older findings with newer ones because the questions of the surveys were differently phrased.

9. Amirault (1997), pp. 10–11.

10. BLS (www.bls.gov).

Chapter 13

1. *Wirtschaftswoche* (2002a).

2. International Centre for Prison Studies (www.kcl.ac.uk/depste/re//icps).

3. Hunt (2003), p. 1.

4. United Nations Office on Drugs and Crime (www.unodc.org).

5. Kestern, Mayhew, and Nieuwbeerta (2000), pp. 25ff. Germany and Italy were not part of this study.

6. BJS (www.ojp.usdoj.gov/bjs) and author's calculations.

7. Rubinstein and Mukamal (2002); and Travis (2002).

8. BJS (www.ojp.usdoj.gov/bjs).

9. Katz and Krueger (1999), pp. 40ff.

Chapter 14

1. United Nations Development Programme (2003), p. 211.

2. OECD (2002), p. 105; and *Wall Street Journal* (2002a).

3. Glied (2003), p. 137; Jones (2002); OECD (2002), p. 99; and OECD Health Data 2002 (CD-ROM).

4. IMS Health database.

5. *Wall Street Journal* (2002a).

6. Murphy and Topel (2000), p. 25; cf. Cutler und McClellan (2001).

7. Ibid., pp. 24, 29; cf. Glied (2003), p. 135.

8. Lichtenberg (2003), p. 20.

9. Lichtenberg (2003a), p. 18.

10. Murphy and Topel (2000), p. 24.

11. *New York Times* (2003).

12. Cf. OECD (2002), p. 107.

13. Jury Verdict Research (www.juryverdictresearch.com).

14. Cf. Howard (2003).

15. AMA (www.ama-assn.org).

16. Ibid.; *Time* (2003); and *USA Today* (2002).

17. Howard (2003).

18. Anderson (1995), p. 2399; JEC (2003); and Kessler and McClellan (1996).

19. Harris Interactive (www.harrisinteractive.com).

20. Kessler and McClellan (1996).

21. Howard (2003).

22. The total cost of health care expenditures in 2000 was about $1,270 billion; the expenditures for prescription drugs were some $150 billion. A tort liability reform that would save $100 billion per annum and halving drug expenditures would together bring about savings of some $175 billion. If those savings were used in their entirety for cost reduction, health care–related expenditures as a share of GDP would have been 11.2 instead of 13.0 percent. (In Germany, the share in 2000 was 10.6 percent.) If the savings had, alternatively, been used for the free supply of health insurance to the uninsured, $4,400 per year per person would have been available—more than enough to cover basic needs. OECD Health Data 2002 (CD-ROM); U.S. Census Bureau (www.census.gov); and author's calculations.

Chapter 15

1. Harris Interactive (www.harrisinteractive.com) and Riquesta. Data for the United States from December 2002, for Germany from June 2003.

2. Bhalla (2002); see also Sala-i-Martin (2002), Sala-i-Martin (2002a), and Fischer (2003).

3. See, for example, Förster and Pearson (2002), p. 35; and Sachverständigenrat zur Begutachtung der gesamtwirtschaftlichen Entwicklung (2002), pp. 350ff.

4. Piketty and Saez (2001), p. 81.

5. Krugman (2002); cf. OECD (2002), p. 142; and Rodrígues, Díaz-Giménez, Quadrini, and Ríos-Rull (2002), p. 12.

6. The measurement of "money income" in the Current Population Survey was changed in 1994. That had the result that from 1993 on, income of low-income earners is shown to be less than before. That, in turn, means a reduction in the dynamism of development of income inequalities, were the current method of measurement used retroactively. Cf. Ilg and Haugen (2000), pp. 29ff.

7. The year 1967 is chosen as the starting point because no older data are available.

8. In the case at hand, a Gini index of the value zero would mean that all Americans earn or consume the same amount. A value of one would mean that all income (or consumption) goes to one American alone—with the rest getting or spending nothing.

9. Just how that discrepancy came to be is not possible to discern. Different methods of calculation could be as much of a reason as the fact that the Gini indexes were created based on incomes *after* taxes.

10. Cf. Eberstadt (2002); and Meyer and Sullivan (2003), p. 19.
11. Meyer and Sullivan (2003), p. 7.
12. Friedman (1957).
13. Aizcorbe, Kennickell, and Moore (2003), pp. 7, 13.
14. Cf. Lucy Lazarony, Credit card companies sidestep usury laws, quoted from www.bankrate.com.
15. Krueger and Perri (2003).
16. Förster and Pearson (2002), p. 10.
17. Bundesministerium der Finanzen (2002), p. 71; and JEC (www.house.gov/jec).
18. Förster and Pearson (2002), p. 30.
19. Tanzi and Schulknecht (2000), pp. 99ff.
20. Ibid., pp. 119, 249.

Chapter 16

1. Cf. Juhn and Murphy (1997), p. 73, and the literature cited there.
2. Card, Lemieux, and Riddell (2003); Council of Economic Advisers (1997), p. 171; Gordon (2000), pp. 3ff.; and OECD (2002), p. 144.
3. Cf. Gordon (2000), p. 5.
4. Cf. Acemoglu (2002), p. 50; and Acemoglu, Aghion, and Violante (2001), p. 5.
5. *Business Week* (2003).
6. Piketty and Saez (2003), pp. 7ff.
7. Ibid.
8. Ibid., pp. 14ff.
9. Gordon (2001), pp. 8ff.
10. Dell (www.dell.com) and *Fortune* (www.fortune.com).
11. *Forbes* (www.forbes.com).
12. Rosen (1981).
13. Cf. Gordon (2001), pp. 8ff.; and Krueger (2002), p. 9.
14. Interview with the Zweites Deutsches Fernsehen, June 13, 2003. Quoted from www.zdf.de.
15. *Handelsblatt* (2003).
16. *Forbes* (2003a).
17. *New Yorker* (2003); and *Wall Street Journal* (2004), p. C3.
18. Krugman (2002).
19. Cf. Gordon (2001), p. 10.
20. *New Yorker* (2003).
21. *Fortune* (2003a).
22. Kennickell (2003), p. 3.
23. Ibid.
24. Kennickell, pp. 5–6.
25. Culp and Niskanen (2003).
26. Council of Economic Advisers (1997), p. 175.
27. Cf. Acemoglu (2002), pp. 7ff.
28. Council of Economic Advisers (1997), pp. 187ff.; and Greenspan (2003a), p. 3.
29. Lerman and Schmidt (1999), p. 33.
30. Greenspan (2000), p. 3.
31. BLS (www.bls.gov).
32. Cf. Greenspan (2000), p. 2; and Mincer and Danninger (2000), p. 2.

33. Cf. Lerman (1997).

34. According to Mincer and Danniger (2000), some 8 to 10 years pass in the United States before an increase in demand for qualified workers results in a greater supply.

35. Cf. Greenspan (2000), p. 2.

36. Cf. Barro (2001), p. 7; Mincer and Danniger (2000), p. 3; and statements by Joseph Stiglitz in *Wirtschaftswoche* (1997).

37. OECD (2003d), p. 54.

38. Ibid., pp. 54, 268.

39. Ibid., p. 167; and author's calculations. For women the gross return was 20.7 percent in the United States, 12.6 percent in France, and 8.5 percent in Germany. No data on Italian women are available.

40. The discrepancy between returns on investments could also come to be because European universities produce less-qualified graduates. There seems to be no evidence that supports such sweeping generalizations.

41. Cf. Acemoglu (2003).

42. Cf. Council of Economic Advisers (2003), p. 115; and Lerman and Schmidt (1999), p. 33.

43. Council of Economic Advisers (1997), p. 170; Förster and Pearson (2002), pp. 15ff.; and Haveman (2000), p. 251.

44. Ibid., pp. 256–57.

Chapter 17

1. Bundesregierung (2001), p. 177.

2. If, however, advances in productivity are fully consumed by the employees, despite high unemployment, job creation is thwarted because unit labor costs remain unchanged.

3. Lerman and Schmidt (1999), p. 33, 46.

4. Federal Reserve Board (www.federalreserve.gov); cf. *Wirtschaftswoche* (2000a).

5. Krugman (1998), p. 36.

6. OECD (2003b), p. 75. According to monthly, seasonally adjusted data published by the U.S. Bureau of Labor Statistics, the share of those who remained unemployed for more than 26 weeks stood at 22.8 percent in January 2004. BLS (www.bls.gov) and author's calculations.

7. OECD (2003b), pp. 74–75.

8. Rolle and van Suntum (1997), p. 90.

9. *Wirtschaftswoche* (2000b).

10. Cf., for instance, Bertola, Blau, and Kahn (2001), p. 196; and Blanchard and Wolfers (2000), p. 2.

11. *Wirtschaftswoche* (1997).

Chapter 18

1. Speech at the Bundestag, June 13, 2002, quoted from www.bundesregierung.de.

2. OECD (2003d), p. 208. Those numbers include expenditures for vocational training. Considering that those expenditures are higher in Europe, the difference in spending on schools increases further still.

3. Max-Planck-Institut für Bildungsforschung (2001), pp. 13ff.

4. Ibid., pp. 40–41.

5. Schnepf (2002), p. 18.

6. OECD (2003d), p. 246.
7. Bundesministerium für Gesundheit und Soziale Sicherung (2002), p. 74.
8. Cf. Krueger (2002), p. 10; and Palacios (2002), pp. 2–3.
9. Friedman (1982), pp. 102ff.; and Palacios (2002), pp. 3ff.
10. OECD (2003d), p. 257.
11. Cf. Lipset (1997), pp. 33, 77ff.
12. Bundesministerium für Bildung und Forschung (2003a), pp. 204–5.
13. Cf. Krämer (2003).
14. Grüske (1994), pp. 93–94.
15. Ibid., p. 121.

Chapter 19

1. The Gallup Organization. In 1990 the number was at 32 percent, in 1996 it was at 33, and in early 2003 it was at 31 percent.
2. Ibid.
3. Cf. Birdsall and Graham (2000), p. 14.
4. Cf. Alesina, Glaesner, and Sacerdote (2001), pp. 26–27; Houtenville (2001), pp. 27ff.; Sawhill (2000), pp. 61ff; and Solon (2002), pp. 61ff.
5. Cf. ibid., pp. 60–61.
6. Schöppner (2002).
7. Alesina, Di Tella, and MacCulloch (2003).

Chapter 20

1. BLS (www.bls.gov).
2. Council of Economic Advisers (2003), p. 116.
3. Speech in the Bundestag, March 14, 2003, quoted from www.bundesregierung.de.
4. TV interview with the Zweites Deutsches Fernsehen, August 12, 2001, quoted from www.bundeskanzler.de.
5. Take Germany, for example: The official statistics both in Germany and in the United States include only mass layoffs. Alternatively, the applications for unemployment benefits could be taken as a measure. One of the problems is that those who merely move from "hidden" unemployment to being openly unemployed are counted in Germany's layoff statistics (see also Chapter 2).
6. BLS (www.bls.gov). In January 1983, the average tenure was 9.5 years for 45- to 54-year-olds and 12.2 years for 55- to 64-year-olds.
7. Farber (2003), pp. 11ff., 21ff. It is furthermore possible that workers lose more than one job in a given three-year period. All numbers are based on the "Displaced Workers Surveys" of the U.S. Census Bureau.
8. Cf. OECD (1999), p. 68.
9. OECD; cf. Scarpetta, Hemmings, Tressel, and Woo (2002), p. 46. Employment protection legislation is surely not the sole factor that explains these differences. But that it contributes significantly to those discrepancies seems likely.
10. Cf. Bertola, Blau, and Kahn (2001), p. 197; and OECD (1999), p. 68.
11. Cf. Bertola, Blau, and Kahn (2001), p. 187.
12. Presumably the effect would be greater for Germany because employment protection legislation there is stricter than the average in the EU (cf. Figure 20.1).

13. Those perceptions were closest at the end of 2001. The reason for that is presumably that Americans were still heavily influenced by the shock of 9/11.

Conclusion

1. Keynes (1963), p. 358.
2. Cf. Figure 17.2.

References

Acemoglu, Daron. 2003. Cross-country inequality trends. *Economic Journal* 113 (February): 121–49.

———. 2002. Technical change, inequality, and the labor market. *Journal of Economic Literature* 60, no. 1 (March): 7–72.

Acemoglu, Daron, Simon Johnson, and James Robinson. 2002. Reversal of fortune: Geography and institutions in the making of the modern world income distribution. *Quarterly Journal of Economics* 117 (November): 1231–94.

Acemoglu, Daron, Philippe Aghion, and Giovanni L. Violante. 2001. Deunionization, technical change and inequality. Carnegie-Rochester Conference Series on Public Policy (February).

Aizcorbe, Ann M., Arthur B. Kennickell, and Kevin B. Moore. 2003. Recent changes in U.S. family finances. *Federal Reserve Bulletin* (January): 1–31.

Alesina, Alberto F., Silvia Ardagna, Giorgio Nicoletti, and Fabio Schiantarelli. 2003. Regulation and investment. CEPR Discussion Paper no. 3851 (March).

Alesina Alberto F., Rafael Di Tella, and Robert MacCulloch. 2003. Inequality and happiness: Are Europeans and Americans different? Unpublished working paper (March).

Alesina, Alberto, Edward Glaeser, and Bruce Sacerdote. 2001. Why doesn't the United States have a European-style welfare state? *Brookings Paper on Economic Activity*, no. 2.

Amirault, Thomas. 1997. Characteristics of multiple jobholders, 1995. *Monthly Labor Review* (March): 9–15.

Anderson, Richard E. 1999. Billions of defense: The pervasive nature of defensive medicine. *Archives of Internal Medicine* 159, no. 8 (November): 2399–2402.

Babeau, André, and Teresa Sbano. 2003. Household wealth in the national accounts of Europe, the United States and Japan. OECD Statistics Working Paper (March).

Baily, Martin Neil. 2003. Information technology and productivity: Recent findings. Presentation at the AEA meetings (January 3).

Barro, Robert J. 2001. Inequality, growth, and investment. In *Inequality and tax policy*, ed. Kevin A. Hasset and R. Glenn Hubbard, 1–38. Washington, DC: AEI Press.

Beck, Ulrich. 1997. Die Deutschen sind zu fleißig. *Süddeutsche Zeitung* (January 23).

Bertola, Guiseppe, Francine D. Blau, and Lawrence M. Kahn. 2001. Comparative analysis of labor market outcomes: Lessons for the United States from international long-run evidence. In Krueger and Solow (2001): 159–218.

Bertrand, Marianne, and Sendhil Mullainathan. 2003. Are Emily and Greg more employable than Lakisha and Jamal? A field experiment on labor market discrimination. NBER Working Paper no. 9873 (July).

Bhalla, Surjit S. 2002. *Imagine there's no country: Poverty, inequality, and growth in the era of globalization.* Washington, DC: Institute for International Economics.

Birdsall, Nancy, and Carol Graham. 2000. Mobility and markets: Conceptual issues and policy questions. In Birdsall and Graham. (2000a): 3–21.

_____ . 2000a. *New markets, new opportunities? Economic and social mobility in a changing world*. Washington, DC: Brookings Institution Press.

Blanchard, Olivier, and Justin Wolfers. 2000. The role of shocks and institutions in the rise of European unemployment: The aggregate evidence. *Economic Journal*, no. 110 (March): 1–33.

Blanchflower, David G., and Andrew J. Oswald. 2004. Well-being over time in Britain and the USA. *Journal of Public Economics* 88, nos. 7–8 (July): 1359–86.

Blank, Rebecca M. 2002. Evaluating welfare reform in the United States. *Journal of Economic Literature* 40, no. 4 (December): 1105–66.

Blinder, Alan S., and Janet L. Yellen. 2001. The fabulous decade: Macroeconomic lessons from the 1990s. In Krueger and Solow (2001): 91–156.

Börsch-Supan, Axel. 2000. Die Furcht vor dem Untergang der Arbeit. Beiträge zur angewandten Wirtschaftsforschung, no. 576. University of Mannheim (March).

Bundesagentur für Arbeit. 2004. Der Arbeitsmarkt in Deutschland: Monatsbericht Dezember 2003. Nuremberg (January).

Bundesministerium der Finanzen. 2002. Monatsbericht März 2002. Berlin (March).

Bundesministerium für Bildung und Forschung. 2003. *Zur technologischen Leistungsfähigkeit Deutschlands*. Berlin (February).

_____ . 2003a. *Grund- und Strukturdaten 2001/2002*. Berlin (April).

Bundesministerium für Gesundheit und Soziale Sicherung. 2002. *Sozialbericht 2001*.

Bundesregierung. 2001. *Lebenslagen in Deutschland: Der erste Armuts- und Reichtumsbericht der Bundesregierung*.

Business Cycle Dating Committee, National Bureau of Economic Research. 2003. The NBER's business-cycle dating procedure (July 17).

Business Week. 2003. Executive pay (April 21): 86ff.

_____ . 2002. The boon behind the bubble (July 15): 38ff.

Caplow, Theodore, Louis Hicks, and Ben J. Wattenberg. 2001. *The first measured century*. Washington, DC: AEI Press.

Card, David, Thomas Limieux, and W. Craig Riddell. 2003. Unionization and wage inequality: A comparative study of the U.S., the U.K., and Canada. NBER Working Paper no. 9473 (February).

Cohen, Jessica, William T. Dickens, and Adam Posen. 2001. Have the new human-resource management practices lowered the sustainable unemployment rate? In Krueger and Solow (2001): 219–59.

Commission of the European Communities. 2002. Germany's growth performance in the 1990's. Economic Paper no. 170 (May).

_____ . 2002a. Draft Joint Employment Report 2002. Brussels (November).

Committee on Ways and Means, U.S. House of Representatives. 2000. *2000 Green Book*. Washington, DC (October 6).

Council of Economic Advisers. 2004. Annual report. In *Economic report of the president*. Washington, DC: Government Printing Office.

_____ . 2003. Annual report. In *Economic report of the president*. Washington, DC: Government Printing Office.

_____ . 1997. Annual report. In *Economic report of the president*. Washington, DC: Government Printing Office.

Cox, W. Michael, and Richard Alm. 1999. *Myths of rich & poor*. New York: Basic Books.

Crafts, Nicholas. 2002. The Solow productivity paradox in historical perspective. CEPR Discussion Paper no. 3142 (January).

References

Crews, Clyde Wayne Jr. 2003. *Ten thousand commandments: An annual snapshot of the federal regulatory state.* Washington, DC: Cato Institute.

Culp, Christopher L., and William A. Niskanen, eds. *Corporate Aftershock: The Public Policy Lessons from the Collapse of Enron and Other Major Corporations.* New York: John Wiley & Sons and Cato Institute, 2003.

Cutler, David M., and Mark McClellan. 2001. Is technological change in medicine worth it? *Health Affairs* 20, no. 5 (September–October): 11–29.

David, Paul A. 1990. The dynamo and the computer: An historical perspective on the modern productivity paradox. *American Economic Review* 80, no. 2 (May): 355–61.

DeKaser, Richard J. 2003. Don't sweat the debt! National City Financial Market Outlook (February).

DeLong, J. Bradford. 2002. Productivity growth in the 2000s. Unpublished working paper, draft 1.2 (March).

———. 2002a. Macroeconomic vulnerabilities in the twenty-first century economy: A preliminary taxonomy. *International Finance* 5, no. 2, pp. 285–309.

Deutsche Bundesbank. 2002. *Monatsbericht September 2002.*

———. 2002a. *Monatsbericht Juni 2002.*

Deutsches Institut für Wirtschaftsforschung. 2004. Grundlinien der Wirtschaftsentwicklung 2004/2005. DIW Wochenbericht 2004, nos. 1–2. Berlin (January).

Djankov, Simoen, Rafael La Porta, Florencio Lopez-de-Silanes, and Andrei Shleifer. 2002. The regulation of entry. *Quarterly Journal of Economics* 117, no. 1 (February): 1–37.

Dynan, Karen, Kathleen Johnson, and Karen Pence. 2003. Recent changes to a measure of U.S. household debt service. *Federal Reserve Bulletin* (October): 417–24.

Eberstadt, Nicholas. 2002. A misleading measure of poverty. *Washington Post* (February 17).

Einblick. 2002. Ewige Neinsager sind keine Meinungsführer. Interview with Michael Sommer (July 22).

Farber, Henry S. 2003. Job loss in the United States, 1981–2001. NBER Working Paper no. 9707 (May).

Feldstein, Martin. 2003. Why is productivity growing faster? Paper presented at the American Economic Association session on the new economy and growth in the United States (January 3).

Field, Alexander. 1980. The relative stability of German and American industrial growth, 1880–1913: A comparative analysis. In *Wachstumszyklen der deutschen Wirtschaft im 19. und 20. Jahrhundert,* ed. Wilhelm Heinz Schröder and Reinhard Spree, 208–32. Stuttgart: Klett-Cotta.

Fischer, Stanley. 2003. Globalization and its challenges. *American Economic Review* 93, no. 2 (May): 1–30.

Forbes. 2003. There's life left in the Valley (July 7): 33ff.

———. 2003a. EDS: Executives don't suffer (April 14): 56.

Förster, Michael, and Mark Pearson. 2002. Income distribution and poverty in the OECD area: Trends and driving forces. *OECD Economic Studies,* no. 34, pp. 7–39.

Fortune. 2003. Power: Do women really want it? (October 13): 80ff.

———. 2003a. Have they no shame? (April 28): 57ff.

Frankfurter Allgemeine Zeitung. 2002. Unfrei ist, wer arm ist. Interview with Guido Westerwelle (April 28).

Freeman, Richard B. 2000. The U.S. economic model at Y2K: Lodestar for advanced capitalism? Special Supplement on Structural Aspects of Unemployment in Canada, *Canadian Public Policy* 26, no. 1 (July): 187–200.

Freund, Caroline L. 2000. Current account adjustment in industrialized countries. Federal Reserve System International Finance Discussion Paper no. 692 (December).

Friedman, Milton. 1982. *Capitalism and freedom.* Chicago: University of Chicago Press.

———. 1957. *A theory of the consumption function.* Princeton, NJ: Princeton University Press.

Garibaldi, Pietro, and Paolo Mauro. 1999. Deconstructing job creation. IMF Working Paper 99/109 (August).

Giersch, Herbert. 1999. Marktökonomik für die offene Gesellschaft. Walter-Adolf-Jöhr Lecture.

Gilder, George. 1993. *Wealth & poverty.* Oakland, CA: ICS Press.

Glied, Sherry. 2003. Health care costs: On the rise again. *Journal of Economic Perspectives* 17, no. 2 (Spring): 125–48.

Gordon, Robert J. 2003. Hi-tech innovation and productivity growth: Does supply create its own demand? NBER Working Paper no. 9437 (January).

———. 2002. Two centuries of economic growth: Europe chasing the American frontier. Paper prepared for the economic historic workshop, Northwestern University (October 17).

———. 2001. Discussion of Deunionization, technical change and inequality, by Daron Acemoglu, Philippe Aghion, and Giovanni L. Violante. Paper prepared for the Carngie-Rochester Conference Series of Public Policy (February).

———. 2000. Interpreting the "one big wave" in U.S. long-term productivity growth. NBER Working Paper no. 7752 (June).

Greenspan, Alan. 2004. Understanding household debt obligations. Remarks at the Credit Union National Association 2004 Governmental Affairs Conference, Washington, DC (February 23).

———. 2003. The Reagan legacy. Remarks at the Ronald Reagan Library, Simi Valley, CA (April 9).

———. 2003a. Aging global population. Testimony before the Special Committee on Aging, U.S. Senate (February 27).

———. 2002. Remarks at the U.S. Department of Labor and American Enterprise Institute conference (October 23).

———. 2000. Structural change in the new economy. Remarks before the National Governor's Association, 92nd Annual Meeting, State College, PA. (July 11).

Grüske, Karl-Dieter. 1994. Verteilungseffekte der öffentlichen Hochschulfinanzierung in der Bundesrepublik Deutschland: Personale Inzidenz im Querschnitt und Längsschnitt. In *Bildung, Bildungsfinanzierung und Einkommensverteilung II,* 71–147. Neue Folge 221. Berlin: Duncker & Humblot.

Gwartney, James, and Robert Lawson. 2003. *Economic freedom of the world: 2003 annual report.* Vancouver: Fraser Institute.

Handelsblatt. 2003. Deutsche Vorstände werden gut bezahlt (April 9).

———. 1998. Zwickel warnt vor dem Vorbild USA (February 5).

Hatzius, Jan. 2003. Financial conditions: A step in the right direction. Goldman Sachs US Economics Analyst no. 03/22 (May 30).

Haveman, Robert. 2000. Poverty and the distribution of economic well-being since the 1960s. In Perry and Tobin (2000): 243–98.

Houtenville, Andrew J. 2001. Income mobility in the United States and Germany: A comparison of two classes of mobility measures using the GSOEP, PSID, and CPS. *Vierteljahreshefte zur Wirtschaftsforschung* 70, no. 1, pp. 59–65.

Howard, Philip K. 2003. Curing health care: Legal malpractice. *Wall Street Journal* (January 27).

Howard, Philip K. 2002. *The collapse of the common good.* New York: Ballentine Books.

Hubbard, R. Glenn. 2002. Productivity in the 21st century. Remarks at the American Enterprise Institute (October 23).

Hunt, Jennifer. 2003. Teen births keep American crime high. NBER Working Paper no. 9632 (April).

Ilg, Randy E., and Steven E. Haugen. 2000. Earnings and employment trends in the 1990s. *Monthly Labor Review* (March): 21–33.

Institut für Arbeitsmarkt- und Berufsforschung. 2004. Der Arbeitsmarkt 2004 und 2005. IAB Kurzbericht no. 5 (March).

International Monetary Fund. 2003. World economic outlook: Growth and institutions. Washington, DC (April).

———. 2002. World economic outlook: Trade and finance (September).

———. 2002a. United States of America: Staff report for the 2002 Article IV Consultation (July).

———. 2001. World economic outlook: The information technology revolution (October).

Jackson, Richard. 2003. Germany and the challenge of global aging. Center for International and Strategic Studies. Washington, DC (March).

Jargowsky, Paul A. 2003. Stunning progress, hidden problems: The dramatic decline of concentrated poverty in the 1990s. Brookings Institution Living Cities Census Series (May).

Joint Economic Committee, U.S. Congress. 2003. Liability for medical malpractice: Issues and evidence (May).

Jones, Charles I. 2002. Why have health expenditures as a share of GDP risen so much? NBER Working Paper no. 9325 (November).

Jorgenson, Dale W., Mun So. Ho, and Kevin Stiroh. 2003. Lessons for Europe from the U.S. growth resurgence. *CESifo Economic Studies* 49, no. 1, pp. 27–47.

Juhn, Chinhui, and Kevin M. Murphy. 1997. Wage inequality and family labor supply. *Journal of Labor Economics* 15, no. 1 (January): 72–97.

Katz, Lawrence F., and Alan B. Krueger. 1999. The high-pressure U.S. labor market of the 1990s. *Brookings Paper on Economic Activity*, no. 1.

Kennickell, Arthur B. 2003. A rolling tide: Changes in the distribution of wealth in the U.S., 1989–2001. Survey of Consumer Finances Working Paper (March).

Kessler, Daniel P., and Mark McClellan. 1996. Do doctors practice defensive medicine? *Quarterly Journal of Economics* 111, no. 2 (May): 353–90.

Kesteren, John van, Pat Mayhew, and Paul Nieuwbeerta. 2000. Criminal victimisation in seventeen industrialised countries: Key findings from the 2000 International Crime Victims Survey. Wetenschappelijk Onderzoek- en Documentatiecentrum, Onderzoek en beleid, no. 187.

Keynes, John Maynard. 1963. Economic possibilities for our grandchildren. In *Essays in persuasion*, 358–73. New York: W.W. Norton.

King, Stephen. 2002. The consumer takes it all: The real winners and losers from the new economy. HSBC Research Paper (May).

Krämer, Walter. 2003. Studiengebühren sind sozial. *Novo*, no. 63 (March–April): 42.

Krueger, Alan B. 2002. Inequality: Too much of a good thing. Unpublished working paper (August 4).

Krueger, Alan B., and Robert M. Solow, eds. 2001. *The roaring nineties: Can full employment be sustained?* New York: Russel Sage Foundation and Century Foundation.

Krueger, Alan B. 2000. Labor policy and labor research since the 1960s: Two ships sailing in orthogonal directions. In Perry and Tobin (2000): 299–332.

Krueger, Dirk, and Krishna B. Kumar. 2004. US-Europe differences in technology-driven growth: Quantifying the role of education. *Journal of Monetary Economics*, no. 51, pp. 161–90.

———. 2002. Skill specific rather than general education: A reason for US-Europe growth differences? NBER Working Paper no. 9408 (December).

Krueger, Dirk, and Fabrizio Perri. 2003. On the welfare consequences of the increase in inequality in the United States. Working paper (June). Forthcoming in *NBER Macroeconomics Annual 2003*, vol. 18. Cambridge, MA: MIT Press.

Krugman, Paul. 2002. For richer, *New York Times Magazine* (October 20): 62ff.

———. 1998. America the boastful. *Foreign Affairs* (May–June): 32–45.

Laubach, Thomas. 2003. New evidence on the interest rate effects of budget deficits and debt. Federal Reserve System Finance and Economics Discussion Series, no. 2003-12 (May).

Lerman, Robert I., and Stephanie R. Schmidt. 1999. An overview of economic, social and demographic trends affecting the U.S. labor market. Report prepared at the Urban Institute for the U.S. Department of Labor. Washington, DC (August).

———. 1997. Meritocracy without rising inequality? Urban Institute *Economic Restructuring and the Job Market*, no. 2 (September).

Lewis, Michael. 2002. In defense of the boom. *New York Times Magazine* (October 27): 44ff.

Lichtenberg, Frank R. 2003. The impact of new drug launches on longevity: Evidence from longitudinal, disease-level data from 52 countries, 1982–2001. NBER Working Paper no. 9754 (June).

———. 2003a. The value of new drugs: The good news in capsule form. *Milken Institute Review* (Fourth quarter): 17–25.

Lipset, Seymour Martin. 1997. *American exceptionalism: A double edged sword.* New York: W.W. Norton.

Maddison, Angus. 2001. *The world economy: A millennial perspective.* OECD Development Centre Studies. Paris.

Malkiel, Burton G. 2003. The efficient market hypothesis and its critics. *Journal of Economic Perspectives* 17, no. 1 (Winter): 59–82.

Martel, Jennifer L. 2000. Reasons for working multiple jobs. *Monthly Labor Review* (October): 42–43.

Mauer, Marc, and Meda Chesney-Lind. 2002. *Invisible punishment: The collateral consequences of mass imprisonment.* New York: W.W. Norton.

Max-Planck-Institut für Bildungsforschung. 2001. Pisa 2000. Zusammenfassung zentraler Befunde. Berlin.

McGuckin, Robert H., and Bert van Ark. 2003. *Performance 2002: Productivity, employment, and income in the world's economies.* New York: The Conference Board.

McKinnon, Jesse. 2003. The black population in the United States: March 2003. U.S. Census Bureau Current Population Report (April).

McKinsey Global Institute. 2001. *U.S. productivity growth 1995–2000: Understanding the contribution of information technology relative to other factors.* Washington, DC (October).

230

Meyer, Bruce D., and James X. Sullivan. 2003. Measuring the well-being of the poor using income and consumption. NBER Working Paper no. 9760 (June).

Mincer, Jacob, and Stephan Danninger. 2000. Technology, unemployment, and inflation. NBER Working Paper no. 7817 (July).

Moore, Michael. 2001. *Stupid white men . . . and other sorry excuses for the state of the nation.* New York: Regan.

Mosisa, Abraham T. 2003. The working poor in 2001. *Monthly Labor Review* (November–December).

Murphy, Kevin M., and Robert Topel. 2000. Medical research: What's it worth? *Milken Institute Review* (First quarter): 23–30.

Naifeh, Mary. 1998. Trap door? Revolving door? Or both? Dynamics of economic well-being, poverty 1993–94. U.S. Census Bureau Household Economic Studies (July).

Natcher, William C. 2002. Debt service burden reconsidered. National City Financial Market Outlook (September).

New Yorker. 2003. Spend! Spend! Spend! (February 17 and 24): 132ff.

New York Times. 2003. Hospitals fearing malpractice crisis (June 3).

Organization for Economic Co-operation and Development. 2004. *Main Economic Indicators.* Paris (February).

———. 2004a. *Main science and technology indicators 2003,* no. 2.

———. 2003. *Economic outlook,* no. 74 (December).

———. 2003a. *OECD employment outlook: Toward more and better jobs* (July).

———. 2003b. *Labour force statistics 1982–2002* (July).

———. 2003c. *The sources of economic growth in OECD countries.*

———. 2003d. *Education at a glance: 2003.*

———. 2002. *OECD economic surveys: United States 2002,* no 18 (November).

———. 2000. *Employment outlook 2000* (June).

———. 2000a. *A new economy? The changing role of innovation and information technology in growth.*

———. 1999. *Employment outlook 1999* (June).

Palacios, Miguel. 2002. Human capital contracts: "Equity-like" instruments for financing higher education. Cato Institute Policy Analysis no. 462 (December 16).

Peach, Richard, and Charles Steindel. 2000. A nation of spendthrifts? An analysis of trends in personal and gross saving. Federal Reserve Bank of New York *Current Issues in Economics and Finance* 6, no. 10 (September): 1–6.

Perry, George L., and James Tobin. 2000. *Economic events, ideas, and policies: The 1960s and after.* Washington, DC: Brookings Institution.

Pew Research Center for the People & the Press. 2003. Views of a changing world. Washington, DC (June).

Piketty, Thomas, and Emmanuel Saez. 2003. Income inequality in the United States, 1913–1998. *Quarterly Journal of Economics* 118, no. 1, pp. 1–39.

Piketty, Thomas, and Emmanuel Saez. 2001. Income inequality in the United States, 1913–1998. NBER Working Paper no. 8467 (September).

Putnam, Robert D. 2000. *Bowling alone: The collapse and revival of American community.* New York: Simon & Schuster.

Roach, Stephen S. 2003. An historic moment? Morgan Stanley Daily Economic Comment (June 23).

———. 1998. Global restructuring: Lessons, myths, and challenges. Morgan Stanley Dean Witter Special Economic Study (June 12).

Rodríguez, Santiago Budría, Javier Díaz-Giménez, Vincenzo Quadrini, and José-Víctor Ríos-Rull. 2002. Updated facts on the U.S. distributions of earnings, income and wealth. Federal Reserve Bank of Minneapolis *Quarterly Review* 26, no. 3 (Summer): 2–35.

Rolle, Carsten, and Ulrich van Suntum. 1997. *Langzeitarbeitslosigkeit im Ländervergleich: zum Einfluß von sozialen Sicherungssystemen und Tariffindungssystemen auf die Beschäftigung in Deutschland, Schweiz, Österreich, und die USA.* Berlin: Duncker und Humblot.

Rosen, Sherwin. 1981. The economics of superstars. *American Economic Review* 71, no. 5 (December): 845–58.

Rubinstein, Gwen, and Debbie Mukamal. 2002. Welfare and housing: Denial of benefits to drug offenders. In Mauer and Chesney-Lind (2002): 37–49.

Sachs, Jeffrey D. 2003. Institutions matter, but not for everything. International Monetary Fund *Finance & Development* 40, no. 2 (June): 38–41.

Sachverständigenrat zur Begutachtung der gesamtwirtschaftlichen Entwicklung. 2003. *Jahresgutachten 2003/04: Staatsfinanzen konsolodieren—Steursystem reformieren.* Stuttgart: Metzler-Poeschel.

———. 2002. *Jahresgutachten 2002/03: Zwanzig Punkte für Beschäftigung und Wachstum.* Stuttgart: Metzler-Poeschel.

Sala-i-Martin, Xavier, 2002. The world distribution of income, estimated from individual country distributions. NBER Working Paper no. 8933 (May).

———. 2002a. The disturbing "rise" of global income inequality. NBER Working no. 8904 (April).

Sanchez, Thomas W., Robert E. Lang, and Dawn Dhavale. 2003. Security versus status? A first look at the Census' gated community data. Metropolitan Institute, Alexandria, VA (July).

Sawhill, Isabel. 2000. Opportunity in the United States: Myth or reality? In Birdsall and Graham (2000a): 22–35.

Scarpetta, Stefano, Philip Hemmings, Thierry Tressel, and Jaejoon Woo. 2002. The role of policy and institutions for productivity and firm dynamics: Evidence from micro and industry data. OECD Economics Department Working Paper no. 329 (April).

Schachter, Jason. 2001. Geographical mobility March 1999 to March 2000. U.S. Census Bureau Current Population Report (May).

Schmidley, Dianne. 2003. The foreign-born population in the United States: March 2002. U.S. Census Bureau Current Population Report (February).

Schneider, Friedrich. 2003. Stellt das Anwachsen der Schattenwirtschaft ein Problem für die Wirtschafts- und Finanzpolitik dar? Einige vorläufige empirische Erkenntnisse. Forthcoming in *Perspektiven der Wirtschaftspolitik: Festschrift zum 65. Geburtstag von Prof. René L. Frey*, ed. Christopher A. Schaltegger and Stefan C. Schaltegger. Zurich: vdf Hochschulverlag.

Schnepf, Sylke Viola. 2002. A sorting hat that fails? The transition from primary to secondary school in Germany. Unicef Innocenti Research Centre Working Paper no. 92 (July).

Schöppner, Klaus-Peter. 2002. Sicherheit garantiert noch keine Zuversicht. *Die Welt* (December 31).

Sinn, Hans-Werner. 2002. Die rote Laterne: Die Gründe für Deutschlands Wachstumsschwäche und die notwendigen Reformen. Ifo-Schnelldienst, no. 55 (December 17).

Solon, Gary. 2002. Cross-country differences in intergenerational earnings mobility. *Journal of Economic Perspectives* 16, no. 3 (Summer): 59–66.

Sorensen, Elaine, and Helen Oliver. 2002. Child support reforms in PRWORA: Initial impacts. Urban Institute Discussion Paper (February).

Der Spiegel. 2003. Mutter aller Gefahren (April 7).

Statistisches Bundesamt. 2003. *Statistisches Jahrbuch 2003 für die Bundesrepublik Deutschland.* Wiesbaden. (September).

———. 2003a. *Leben und Arbeiten in Deutschland: Ergebnisse des Mikrozensus 2002* (June).

———. 2002. *Statistisches Jahrbuch für die Bundesrepublik Deutschland* (September).

———. 2002a. *Statistisches Jahrbuch für das Ausland* (September).

Stinson, John F. Jr. 1997. New data on multiple jobholding available from the CPS. *Monthly Labor Review* (March): 3–8.

———. 1990. Multiple jobholding up sharply in the 1980's. *Monthly Labor Review* (July): 3–10.

Süddeutsche Zeitung. 2003. Das Zitat (January 14).

Summers, Lawrence H., and J. Bradford DeLong. 2002. Anatomy of the Nasdaq crash. Syndizierter Zeitungsaufsatz (April 20). Quoted from www.j-bradford-delong.net.

———. 2002a. New rules for the new economy? Syndizierter Zeitungsaufsatz (April 20). Quoted from www.j-bradford-delong.net.

Tagesspiegel. 2002. Was für den Aktienkurs gut ist, ist auch gut für die Mitarbeiter. Interview with Kajo Neukirchen (March 6).

Tanzi, Vito, and Ludger Schuknecht. 2000. *Public spending in the 20th century: A global perspective.* Cambridge: Cambridge University Press.

Time. 2003. The doctor won't see you now (June 9): 46ff.

Travis, Jeremy. 2002. Invisible punishment: An instrument of social exclusion. In Mauer and Chesney-Lind (2002): 15–36.

Triplett, Jack E., and Barry P. Bosworth. 2003. Productivity measurement issues in service industries: "Baumol's disease" has been cured. FRBNY *Economic Policy Review* (September): 23–33.

UBS Warburg. 2003. U.S. Economic Perspectives (May 2).

———. 2002. U.S. Economic Perspectives (November 15).

United Nations. 2002. *World Population Ageing 1950–2050.* New York.

United Nations Development Programme. 2003. *Human development report 2003: Millennium development goals: a compact among nations to end human poverty.*

USA Today. 2002. Fed-up obstetricians look for a way out (July 1).

U.S. Bureau of Labor Statistics. 2004. Consumer expenditures in 2002. Report no. 974 (February).

———. 2003. Comparative real gross domestic product per capita and per employed person: Fourteen countries, 1960–2002. Washington, DC (July).

———. 2003a. Characteristics of Minimum Wage Workers: 2002.

———. 2003b. Highlights of Women's Earnings in 2002 (September).

———. 2002. Twenty-first century moonlighters. *Issues in Labor Statistics* 2002, no. 7.

U.S. Census Bureau. 2003. Income in the United States: 2002. Washington DC (September).

———. 2003a. Poverty in the United States: 2002 (September).

———. 2002. *Statistical abstracts of the United States: 2002.* Washington, DC: Government Printing Office.

U.S. Chamber of Commerce. 2004. Employee benefits study 2003. Washington, DC (January).

———. 2003. Digital economy 2003 (December).

———. 2002. Digital economy 2002 (February).

U.S. Department of Education. 2003. The condition of education 2002 (June).

U.S. Department of Labor. 2001. Report on the American workforce.

Vedder, Richard K., and Lowell E. Gallaway. 1997. *Out of work: Unemployment and government in twentieth-century America.* New York: New York University Press.

Wall Street Journal. 2004. Jurors begin deliberating fate of Tyco's Kozlowski and Swartz (March 19).

————. 2002. Tech will be back, past slumps suggest, as innovators revive it (October 18).

————. 2002a. Drug makers fight to fend off cuts in European prices (June 7).

————. 2001. As officials lost faith in the minimum wage, Pat Williams lived it (July 19).

Washington Post. 2003. The shift (March 23).

Wasmer, Etienne. 2003. Interpreting European and US labour market differences: The specificity of human capital investments. CEPR Discussion Paper no. 3780 (January).

Wirtschaftswoche. 2002. Frustriert oder ruiniert (July 18): 50ff.

————. 2002a. Perspektiven (February 14): 166.

————. 2001. Turbulenzen, Rückschläge, Zufälle. Interview with Alvin Toffler (June 14): 59.

————. 2001a. Jeder Penny zählt (September 6): 78ff.

————. 2000. www (February 10): 82ff.

————. 2000a. Länger warten (September 14): 56ff.

————. 2000b. Erster richtiger Job (February 24): 52ff.

————. 1997. Egalitärer geht es nicht. Interview with Joseph Stiglitz (December 4): 44.

World Health Organization. 2003. The world health report 2003: Shaping the future. Geneva (October).

World Bank. 2003. *World Development Indicators 2003.* Washington, DC.

Wright, Erik Olin, and Rachel E. Dwyer. 2003. The patterns of job expansions in the USA: A comparison of the 1960s and 1990s. *Socio-Economic Review* 2003, no. 1, pp. 289–325.

Wu, Ximing, Jeffrey M. Perloff, and Amos Golan. 2002. Effects of government policies on income distribution and welfare. University of California Institute of Industrial Relations Working Paper (February).

Yergin, Daniel, and Joseph Stanislaw. 2002. *The commanding heights: The battle for the world economy.* New York: Touchstone.

Index

Page references followed by the letter f or t refer to figures and tables respectively.

About the Author

Olaf Gersemann is the foreign news editor for *Financial Times Deutschland*. Prior to that, he was the Washington correspondent for *Wirtschaftswoche*, Germany's largest economic and business weekly. Before joining *Wirtschaftswoche* in 1996, he studied economics at Cologne University and Trinity College, Dublin, and worked for the German financial daily *Handelsblatt*. In 2001, Gersemann was awarded the Ludwig Erhard Prize, the most prestigious German economic reporting prize for journalists under the age of 35.

Cato Institute

Founded in 1977, the Cato Institute is a public policy research foundation dedicated to broadening the parameters of policy debate to allow consideration of more options that are consistent with the traditional American principles of limited government, individual liberty, and peace. To that end, the Institute strives to achieve greater involvement of the intelligent, concerned lay public in questions of policy and the proper role of government.

The Institute is named for *Cato's Letters*, libertarian pamphlets that were widely read in the American Colonies in the early 18th century and played a major role in laying the philosophical foundation for the American Revolution.

Despite the achievement of the nation's Founders, today virtually no aspect of life is free from government encroachment. A pervasive intolerance for individual rights is shown by government's arbitrary intrusions into private economic transactions and its disregard for civil liberties.

To counter that trend, the Cato Institute undertakes an extensive publications program that addresses the complete spectrum of policy issues. Books, monographs, and shorter studies are commissioned to examine the federal budget, Social Security, regulation, military spending, international trade, and myriad other issues. Major policy conferences are held throughout the year, from which papers are published thrice yearly in the *Cato Journal*. The Institute also publishes the quarterly magazine *Regulation*.

In order to maintain its independence, the Cato Institute accepts no government funding. Contributions are received from foundations, corporations, and individuals, and other revenue is generated from the sale of publications. The Institute is a nonprofit, tax-exempt, educational foundation under Section 501(c)3 of the Internal Revenue Code.

CATO INSTITUTE
1000 Massachusetts Ave., N.W.
Washington, D.C. 20001
www.cato.org